PROPERTY OF
ARAB PUBLIC LIBRARY

The Wonderful World of Mammals

by the same author

Going to the Zoo with Roger Caras

The Wonderful World of Mammals

Adventuring with Stamps

by ROGER CARAS

Harcourt Brace Jovanovich, Inc. / New York

Printed in the United States of America

First edition
B C D E F G H I J K

Library of Congress Cataloging in Publication Data

Caras, Roger A
The wonderful world of mammals.

SUMMARY: Introduces forty-one mammals using postage stamps of animals from many countries as illustrations.
1. Mammals–Juvenile literature. 2. Postage-stamps–Topics–Mammals.
[1. Mammals. 2. Postage-stamps–Topics–Mammals] I. Title.
QL706.2.C37 599 73-5235
ISBN 0-15-299300-2

For Roberta, who has made so much happen . . .

Contents

Preface

If you want to find two words that really get people all mixed up, you can't do very much better than *animal* and *mammal.* One way of making it clear is to say that all mammals are animals, but all animals aren't mammals. A mammal is just one kind of animal, just as birds, snakes, fish, and insects are other kinds.

Although there are some germs that can confuse matters, it is pretty safe to say that everything that lives on planet Earth is either a plant or an animal. If someone looks surprised when you say that an ant or a sparrow is an animal, remind them that they are more closely related to a horse than they are to a cabbage!

What makes a mammal a mammal? There are several different ways to tell a mammal from the other kinds of animals you might see. All mammals have hair or fur at some stage of their lives. Mammals are all air breathers, and none can live without it for long. Even the great whales that live in the sea must come to the surface to breathe and cannot stay down like fish. With a few rare exceptions (the duck-billed platypus and the spiny anteater from Australia and New Guinea), all mammals give birth to living young. They do not lay eggs the way birds, insects, some reptiles, and many fish do. And finally there is the one characteristic that is common to all mammals and gives them their name. Mammals feed their young with mammae or breasts. Without their mother's milk, young mammals would soon die.

Other kinds of animals have hair (spiders), other kinds give birth to living young (many fish and reptiles), and some are very good parents (many birds), but no animals except *mammals* actually feed their young with a mother's milk.

This book is about mammals. A mammal wrote it, and only a mammal can read it, for only one animal on Earth has developed what we call higher intelligence and he is the mammal called man.

Being a man carries certain very important responsibilities with it. We are the lucky animals because we can read a book, listen to music and appreciate it, and organize our activities into things like team sports. But because we have risen to the top of the animal tree, it is up to us to care for all the other animals.

Many of the animals whose pictures you will see on stamps may not be here very long unless we try to help them survive. We have already taken away too much of their native habitats and shot too many of them for foolish reasons—like skins. We cannot go on the way we have been going, not for too much longer, or we will make the Earth—home of all mammals—a very sad and lonely place.

So, when we think of mammals, we should think of intelligence, and when we think of intelligence, we should think of responsibility. They go together and can never be viewed apart—not if we really care what happens to wildlife, to our planet, and to ourselves.

It is interesting that man should picture animals so often on his stamps. It is almost as if he had a guilty conscience. He puts animals on stamps next to the pictures of kings and queens and his greatest monuments. It is almost as if man, the intelligent mammal, were saying to all his fellow mammals, "Forgive me." Every time we get a letter with an animal stamp on it, perhaps we should think of that, feel a little guilty, and vow to try harder. It would be very sad indeed if the only animals left a few decades from now were on stamps. They are pretty there, but they belong in life, too, in forest, jungle, swamp, and desert—where it was intended that they be.

Introduction

Just about everybody collects stamps sometime during his lifetime. It is sad, but true, that many people lose interest in their collections by the time they become adults. Perhaps it is because they find more interesting things to do, or perhaps it is because once they fill in the easy places in their albums, they become discouraged. "I could never fill my whole album," they say, "so why try?"

A good way to prevent this kind of discouragement is through the marvelous world of *topical stamp collecting*. Topical collecting simply means that you pick a subject that interests you instead of a country or group of countries. You then make up your own albums and set about gathering and displaying stamps that tell stories of things that interest you personally. You can collect stamps about sports, kings, or children, stamps about music, animals, just birds alone, famous explorers, airplanes, famous ships, or just about anything else that comes to your mind. It can be very exciting and can supply wonderful hours of learning and adventure for your whole life.

I would like to share with you some stamp adventures from my own animal stamp collection. Perhaps you will want to start a topical collection of your own. All you need to begin is interest in a subject and the love of beautiful things. From there on it is all adventure.

You are probably going to have to learn a little more about animals than you now know in order to organize your collection properly. Your librarian or teacher can help you locate a good animal encyclopedia that you will need to refer to from time to time. Also, a new, up-to-date atlas is really a necessity to find out the countries that your stamps come from, and all good libraries have them.

You will notice some confusion in spelling—in your own collection and on the pages that follow. When we refer to a country, we use its English name, but that isn't the name used in that country. Deutschland is the German name for Germany, and Magyar is Hungarian for Hungary. There are lots of countries where only a few letters change—Fujeira and Fujairah for example—and others where the word is entirely different. It is easy in this book because we tell you where each stamp comes from, but as you build your own collection—no matter what subject you decide to specialize in—you will have to learn to recognize foreign words yourself.

You will find that your collection becomes a whole school in itself—you learn language, geography, biology—and lessons learned this way are lessons that remain with you all your life. If you make it a rule *never* to place a stamp in your collection until you have located its country of origin on a map, you will find you probably know more about geography than anyone else in your family. If you understand each animal, too, you will know learn a great deal of zoology. Just think how you will impress everyone the next time you go to the zoo. Stamp collecting is the fun way to learn about your world. I hope you decide to try it.

When you see the sign below in this book, it means the animal is an endangered one—one that will disappear unless we do everything in our power to protect those that are left and the habitat they live in.

The Wonderful World of Mammals

The Lion *(Panthera leo)*

King of the Jungle?

When Kenya, Uganda, and Tanganyika were under British rule, many beautiful stamps appeared picturing the wondrous wildlife of Africa. This stamp showing Queen Elizabeth II and a stately male lion was printed between 1954 and 1959.

This 1963 stamp from colorful India shows one of the few lions left in the Gir Forest region. These animals are rare, and no one is allowed to hunt them.

French Equatorial Africa was a humid area of nearly 1,000,000 square miles in western Africa. In 1958, it was divided into four republics—Chad, Congo, Gabon, and the Central African Republic (formerly Ubangi-Shari). This 1957 stamp shows both a lion and a lioness.

Up until 1941 two parts of the Portuguese colony of Mozambique, Manica and Sofala, hot and humid areas in southeastern Africa, were known as the Mozambique Company and issued their own stamps. This triangular stamp showing a male lion resting appeared in 1937.

(Asiatic lion only) VANISHING ANIMAL

"King of the jungle," they call him, but although that is an exciting legend to think about when you see a lion in the circus or zoo, it is not true.

The mighty lion is not afraid of many things, but he is not very kinglike when an elephant wants to pass his way. Even a couple of very determined-looking water buffalo can convince just about any sensible lion to pick up his family and move off to another part of Africa.

Not only does the lion fail as a king, but he doesn't even come from the jungle! The African lion is a cat of the open plains—high, dry country known as savanna—and is much more likely to turn up in a desert than in a jungle. He will gladly curl up for a nap in the shade of a clump of trees, he will even go into a forest, but the steaming jungle with water running off every leaf is not for him. At one time he ranged up through the arid regions of the Middle East as far as Europe, but in modern times he has been found mostly in Africa south of the great, burning Sahara Desert and in a few places in northwestern India.

Lions travel in family groups known as *prides*. Sometimes two families will be found together, and the pride will number a dozen or more individuals. Since lions are very good parents, it is quite common to see the young of two different litters in the same pride. The parents take endless abuse from their young, who can't seem to learn that tails and ears aren't for chewing. Even the most frolicsome bunch of cubs can be brought to a dead standstill, however, by one throat rumble from either parent.

If you were to travel all the way around the world with just one purpose in mind—to see the wild cats of the world in their homes—the chances are that the lion is the only success you would have. Almost all wild cats are very secretive. At the first sign of man they slink away and disappear into the forest or the jungle. Not so the lion. If he is well fed, it is almost impossible to get him to move until he is either thirsty or hungry again. In many of the game preserves and parks in Africa, you can drive right up to a pride of lions during the midday heat and hardly get the animals to look your way.

When a lion is well fed, even the animals he normally preys upon will ignore him. Zebras, gazelles, wart hogs—all will come to a water hole when the lion is drinking and settle down to drink only a few feet off. Let a lion announce that he is hungry, though, and the picture is very much different.

A well-fed lion, it should be noted, is a lion who has a good hunting lioness in his pride. Strange as it may seem, the lion seldom kills his own food unless traveling alone. Instead, he will stand at the edge of a broad plain and give a mighty roar. Once he has stampeded the herds of hoofed animals, he will go back and take another nap. The frightened animals will run right into the females, who quietly moved around behind the herd before the male gave his roar. They will make the kill, but the mighty lord will awake from his nap in time to take the best morsels for himself.

The Giraffe *(Giraffa camelopardalis)*

The Tallest Animal in the World

Nyassa was part of Portuguese East Africa and has not issued stamps since 1925. This stamp appeared in 1901 and pictures a giraffe in a typical pose, browsing among the top branches of a tall tree.

This 1954–1959 stamp from Kenya, Uganda, and Tanganyika also shows an adult giraffe browsing where he has no competition. We can understand why nature gave the giraffe his extraordinary design when we watch him feed.

In 1937 the Mozambique Company pictured this handsome giraffe in the open flat country where he is still to be found towering over all the other creatures of the land. Happily the giraffe seems to survive. He is so regal-looking that even hunters aren't anxious to shoot him.

This 1959 stamp from the Belgian Congo, one of the last stamps issued before the Congo achieved its independence from Belgium, pictures an adult giraffe in a pose that makes one feel he is just about to run. He seems alert to danger and appears to be carefully surveying his surroundings.

The giraffe is a pretty unlikely-looking creature. A big male giraffe can weigh as much as two tons, and a great deal of that is neck. A full-grown specimen can be nearly twenty feet tall. Nature evidently gave the giraffe such extreme height because his favorite food is the young leaves and shoots of the acacia tree. Since he is the tallest animal in the world, he has no competition. He has the pasture of the treetops all to himself.

The giraffe's extremely long legs and neck make eating easy, but they make drinking a problem. In order to get his mouth down to where the water is, the giraffe must spread his legs far apart and lower his head to ground level at the end of his telephone pole-like neck. Once in the drinking position, he is easy prey for his most troublesome enemy, the lion. He cannot recover his standing position very quickly, so the lion has a good opportunity to make his kill. When he is upright, the giraffe is more than a match for the lion. Because of his great height and suspicious nature, he is almost impossible to sneak up on. A big giraffe can run as fast as thirty-two miles an hour and keep it up long after a lion has quit and lies panting in the dust. The giraffe's powerful front legs are very good weapons. Woe to the lion that gets hit by one!

Giraffes are generally very timid. They are quiet and go out of their way not to interfere with other animals. Just about all they ask is to be allowed to mind their own business. That business consists of eating and drinking in the morning and in the evening and sleeping during the heat of day. Giraffes can sleep while standing up, but if there are no lions on the prowl, they seem to prefer to lie down in the deep grass and have a really good rest.

A giraffe herd usually has a wise old male in charge, with cows and calves tagging obediently along. A herd can number anywhere from twelve to seventy individual animals, but the larger numbers are seldom seen. Young males are tolerated as long as they don't challenge the old bull's authority. If a young male feels it is time to take over, he must fight the old-timer, and that can be a brutal affair. Giraffes fight by hitting each other with the two blunt horns that rise out of the top of their heads and the knob that can usually be seen just about between the eyes. That head, when swung at the end of that long, powerful neck, really hits hard, and sometimes permanent damage is done.

It takes a mother giraffe as long as fourteen or fifteen months to have her single calf. Occasionally, twins are born, but that is really quite unusual. A baby weighs between 100 and 150 pounds when born and can stand within twenty minutes. Within an hour he starts to nurse and keeps it up for nine months. A giraffe lives to be about twenty years old unless careless about lions or unfortunate enough to meet a hunter with a gun and not enough love for the beautiful creatures of the world.

The Polar Bear (*Thalarctos maritimus*)

White Monarch of the North

In this 1953 stamp from Canada (the other stamps in the set are the moose and the bighorn sheep, seen elsewhere in this book), the handsome and aloof head of a polar bear is shown against some ice ridges. Holding his head high and alert is a characteristic pose of this great hunter.

This Greenland stamp picturing a polar bear moving across an ice field first appeared in 1938. *Surcharged* or *overprinted* with a new value, it appeared again in 1956. This great Danish province in the North Atlantic Ocean has fewer than 47,000 people living on an island over 800,000 square miles in area. That means an area more than five times as great as California doesn't have as many people as a small California town.

In 1956 the German Democratic Republic (East Germany) issued a set of six stamps to publicize the Berlin Zoo. The other animals depicted are elephants, flamingos, a rhinoceros, a deer, and a bison. The highest value in the set is this stamp picturing a polar bear.

The Russians frequently picture wildlife on their stamps. This example from a 1964 wildlife set shows a polar bear sitting back on his haunches and gives a good view of his "Roman" nose.

The polar bear is the second largest meat-eating land animal left on this planet. Many of the great whales, of course, are very much bigger, but among those meat-eating animals that walk on the land surfaces, only the great brown bear of the islands off the Alaskan coast is taller or heavier. A full-grown male polar bear can be between ten and eleven feet tall when he stands on his hind legs and can weigh more than three-quarters of a ton. That is three times as big as the common black bear we see in our own national parks!

The bears of the world are *omnivorous*, which means that they eat just about everything. In that sense they are like human beings. The polar bear, however, does not get much of a chance to eat anything but meat since he lives only in the extreme Far North where there is very little plant life to feed on. Other bears can rely on honey, berries, roots, and insects as well as hundreds of kinds of flowers and grasses; the great white hunter of the North could not survive without seals. He will feed on an occasional dead whale that he encounters, and he will fish, catch Arctic birds, and seek out the lemming, a small mouselike animal, during the summer, but the seal is the most important item in the polar bear's diet.

One of the reasons the polar bear is white—perhaps the most important reason—is that he hunts the seal out on the open ice. If he were black or brown like his southern cousins, he would be too easy to see and would soon die of starvation. Only the lighter colored bears survive to reproduce their kind, and that is how nature made and keeps her great northern hunter white.

The skin of the polar bear makes a warm blanket and a very handsome rug. For this reason the human hunters of the great northlands, the Eskimos, have hunted the white bear for their own use and for trade. The polar bear is a wise hunter himself, though, and not easy to trick. He is also extremely powerful and doesn't have a very pleasant personality. In the old days not too many polar bears were killed, and many Eskimos were seriously injured, and some killed, just taking those few. Now, however, since the Eskimo hunts with powerful rifles that keep him well out of range of the polar bear's jaws and powerful front legs, often from powerboats that skirt the ice floes and inlets and even at times from low-flying airplanes, the polar bear appears to be doomed. Although it will be a long time before the last white bear is killed in the last outpost near the North Pole, the species is in danger and will rapidly vanish unless steps are taken to protect it.

Polar bear cubs, like all bear cubs around the world, are born in the middle of winter. The birth of the mother's one or two cubs takes place in a cave in the ice and snow, and the offspring do not come out into the world before March. When a mother polar bear has her cubs with her, she is particularly ferocious, and it is very unwise for any creature —including the mighty male—to come near. She has to be stern, for she knows that a male polar bear will kill any cubs he encounters, even his own, and eat them.

The Mighty Gorilla (*Gorilla gorilla*)

The Greatest of the Great Apes

In east-central Africa there is a small area of less than 21,000 square miles bounded by the Congo, Uganda, and Tanzania. At various times in history, the area has been known as German East Africa and Belgian East Africa. Finally, the United Nations established it as a protectorate. In 1959 a handsome set of animal stamps appeared including this wonderful study of an adult gorilla. It is one of the few times the gorilla has appeared on a stamp. In 1965, three years after part of the United Nations protectorate of Ruanda-Urundi became the independent nation of Royaume du Burundi, the same set of animal stamps was overprinted with the new name. It is interesting to trace the political fortunes and misfortunes of a country by watching its stamps. (The country has now become the Republic of Burundi.)

This is an example of how not to show an animal on a stamp. This 1964 stamp from the Republic of Gabon is totally dishonest. The gorilla looks like a hairy man and is shown as ferocious. That is legend—the gorilla is a mild-mannered animal most of the time.

This gorilla on a 1971 Congo stamp is well done. The pose is typical of this greatest of the apes, and the face is natural. Compare this with the stamp from Gabon and see honesty and dishonesty side by side.

This stamp from Fujairah, one of the United Arab Emirates on the eastern Arabian Peninsula, is designed for collectors, not mailing. It shows two gorillas—one much better done than the other. Which do you think looks right? For me, the gorilla on the left looks odd—like a freak of some kind. The gorilla on the right, in the background, is very well done.

If you were to look through all the books in your library to see what they had to say about the gorilla, you would find a surprisingly large number mention the animal but surprisingly few tell you what he is really like. He is such a fearsome-looking brute that many writers have gone on to say wild and exciting things about him without knowing or caring about his true nature.

The gorilla is a very mild-mannered animal that rarely goes out of his way to bother anybody. As a matter of fact, the average gorilla will do just about anything to avoid trouble. He is much too fond of eating and sleeping to waste his time on anything as foolish as fighting. Gorillas are also thought to be very bright, though no one really knows just how smart they are.

A male gorilla can stand between five and six feet tall, and while he may be a little shorter than the average man, he is much heavier. He can weigh almost six hundred pounds, and when he spreads his arms wide, the distance from fingertip to fingertip is greater than his height.

With his high, pointed crown, his flaring nostrils, deep, dark eyes, and massive chest, the gorilla is as fearsome-looking as any creature in the world. He apparently knows it because, although he doesn't like to fight, he doesn't object to scaring other animals, including man, with terrible displays of ferocious temperament. But it is all a big show. He pounds his chest with his fists, raps on the ground with his huge, knobby knuckles, screams like a creature gone mad, tears up plants and throws them all about, and finally charges in the direction of the intruder. If the intruder stands his ground and doesn't run away, the chances are that the gorilla will stop short and go through it all over again. If the intruder still holds his ground, the gorilla will probably wander off into the thick forest muttering to himself. If another gorilla gets close to him at times like this, he is likely to whack out at him. But he is soon over his temper tantrum and settles down to eating and sleeping again as if nothing had happened at all.

Gorillas seldom attack human beings, but on those rare occasions when they carry their threat through, they do not run about on their hind legs. They stay down on all fours, using their front knuckles for support. They bite when in close quarters or slap out with their massive hands. Either way, a gorilla can deliver harsh punishment.

Gorillas are *vegetarians*—they eat nothing but plant food in the wild. They have many favorites, and they are extremely fussy eaters. They like tender young leaves and shoots, and they love the stalks of certain wild plants. In some areas they take a liking to crops being raised by the local farmers and have to be driven out of the fields. Mostly, though, they stay far away from man and his works.

All gorillas come from Africa—two rather widely separated forested regions, one in western Africa and one in the central part. In the past, a great many hunters evidently thought themselves especially brave if they could kill a gorilla, and their numbers were seriously reduced. It is now against the law to hunt them at all, and those that are left will probably have enough young to continue their species.

The Numbat (*Myrmecobius fasciatus*)

The Rare and the Innocent

Not only common animals are shown on postage stamps. This 1959–1961 issue from Australia pictures the rare and unusual numbat or banded anteater. Encountering strange animals like this on stamps in a topical collection and being forced to look them up to see what they are is one of the ways a good stamp collection can educate as well as entertain.

The numbat has appeared on a stamp only once and probably will never be seen again, but lots of his relatives have been pictured more often. The numbat is a marsupial, and here are two of his kin who are better known—the great gray kangaroo from Australia on a handsome Polish stamp of 1972 and a tree kangaroo from the island of New Guinea on this lovely 1971 stamp from Papua New Guinea (formerly called Papua and New Guinea). The study of one animal in our fauna or wildlife collection can lead us on to the study of others.

VANISHING ANIMAL

In southern and southwestern Australia, in those places where the jam tree and the white gum grow, you can sometimes find an occasional numbat or banded anteater. He is such an inoffensive little creature that if you catch one, he won't even struggle or try to bite, although he has more teeth than any other mammal native to Australia, fifty-two altogether. All he will do as you carry him off is give a snuffling grunt or two to tell you how unhappy he is.

When man first arrived in Australia from Europe, he found the strangest collection of mammals anywhere on earth. Almost all of them were marsupials, mammals that do not fully develop their young inside the mother but give birth to them while they are still embryos, only partially developed into forms that look like their parents. The American opossum is a marsupial, and it takes sixteen opossum babies to fill a teaspoon!

One of the strange marsupials the Europeans found was the numbat, and although he wasn't very interesting to hunt, man pushed him toward extinction in another way. Wherever man goes, he takes his pets with him, his domestic dogs and cats. Wherever man's ships go, less petlike animals also travel: the brown rats and house mice that infest every land on earth except, perhaps the Antarctic, were originally hidden passengers on ships sailing to all ports of the world.

Dogs, cats, and rats together have proven to be too much for many shy creatures who were wiped out before having a chance to develop the means of competing. The squirrel-sized numbat is just such a victim. Dogs and cats run wild, either lost or abandoned, and the numbats of the world must pay the penalty. It will not be too much longer before the last banded anteater will be gone.

Not very much is known about the numbat's private life. With his pointed snout and long sticky tongue, he apparently feeds on white ants, swallowing them whole as they are swept into his mouth. He doesn't climb trees, although he seems to live most often in fairly heavy woods. He has a flattened rump and a flattened head, which makes it easier for him to crawl into tight places in and under fallen logs. He is sometimes caught and killed in these hideaways by brush fires that sweep across his homeland.

It is believed that the average numbat mother has four young at a time, and since she does not have a pouch as do some of the other marsupials like the kangaroo, the young must hang onto their mother's coarse hair when they travel about.

The people of Australia are well aware of the fact that many of their wild creatures are few in number and found nowhere else on this planet. They are trying to protect those that are left, those that survived the greed and foolishness of the early settlers. Perhaps the funny little numbat will be one that will make it. Surely, it will be a better world with numbats than without.

The Rhinoceros (*Ceratotherium* and *Diceros*)

Nearsighted and Short-tempered

This 1946 stamp from what was formerly called French Equatorial Africa shows an adult two-horned rhinoceros in profile and a large snake, probably a python. The design was used many times after its first year of issue.

This 1937 triangular stamp from the Mozambique Company shows an adult rhinoceros down on the ground. It is hard to tell if the great creature is sleeping, mud-wallowing, or is the victim of some hunter's gun.

The great South African wild animal set of 1954 includes the wart hog, lion, gnu, leopard, zebra, elephant, hippopotamus, kudu, springbok, gemsbok, nyala, giraffe, sable antelope, and this rhinoceros. He appears to be the square-lipped or white rhinoceros.

This handsome 1959 stamp from the former Belgian colony in west-central Africa shows a handsome bull rhinoceros passing in profile. Somehow this portrait conveys the power of the mighty creature. This stamp is another one of the wildlife set that appeared just before the end of Belgian control in the Congo.

VANISHING ANIMAL

In all the world today there are just five different kinds of rhinoceroses left. In ages long past there were many times that number. The largest land mammal ever known, *Baluchitherium*, was one of these ancient rhinoceroses.

Today there are two Indian rhinoceroses, both with one horn and both with skin that hangs in great folds, which makes them look as if they were wearing armor. The smaller of the two, the so-called sondaicus, has been so badly pressed that there are probably fewer than fifty left in the entire world, all restricted to a few swampy areas in Java. The larger Indian one-horned rhinoceros is a little better off and is still found in parts of Nepal and northeastern India.

The smallest rhinoceros in the world is the Asiatic two-horned rhinoceros found in Burma, Indo-China, Malaysia, Sumatra, and Borneo. Like his one-horned cousin, he seems to be in trouble, and unless hunters observe the law and leave him in peace, the last of his kind may vanish during our lifetime.

In Africa there is a white rhinoceros and a black rhinoceros, at least those are their names. The white rhinoceros is not white, however, and the black is not black. The black is actually yellowish brown, and the white is a yellowish brown with tones of slaty gray. It can be a bit confusing because they both have two horns. It helps to know that the white is the larger of the two (as a matter of fact, he is the second largest land animal left in the world, being second, of course, to the elephant). The white also has a broader snout than the black and is sometimes called the square-lipped rhinoceros for that reason.

The danger from a rhinoceros has been rather overdone by adventure story writers. While a white rhinoceros is a large fellow (he can be six and a half feet tall at the shoulder and can weigh up to four tons), he isn't as dangerous as one might think. Like so many other wild animals, he tends to be a big bluff. The somewhat smaller black rhinoceros (about five feet at the shoulder and two tons in weight) is a bit more aggressive and is more likely to call your bluff and carry through with his charge.

All the rhinoceroses have very bad eyesight, which seems to make them short-tempered. When they catch the scent of a human being, they cast about, snorting and snuffling, and may or may not make a short, threatening charge. Their hearing and their sense of smell are both very keen and more than make up for the curse of bad vision, and they are amazingly fast on their feet.

Many people in the Orient have believed for centuries that the horn of the rhinoceros has magic properties when ground up into a fine powder, and tens of thousands of innocent animals have been killed to feed this silly superstition.

Rhinoceroses do not reproduce very rapidly. Usually only one baby is born, and it takes the mother up to a year and a half to produce it. This is one good reason for restricting the hunting of these beasts.

The Seal, the Sea Lion, and the Walrus (Pinnipedia)

The Fin-footed Ones

This Bulgarian stamp of 1961 pictures a strange creature called *Pelagius monachus.* The animal is apparently some kind of sea lion, but the specific name given on the stamp does not refer to any known species. There is an interesting error here and would make a nice mystery for someone to track down.

This recent Russian stamp pictures what appears to be one of the three races of the northern fur seal. The slaughter of this valuable animal used to go on unchecked, but it is now more carefully controlled. The year of issue was 1960, and the companion stamps show the pike perch and the lake salmon. Earlier, in 1959, very similar stamps appeared picturing the sturgeon and a salmon.

Ecuador issued the first stamps for the province of the Galapagos Islands (Columbus Archipelago) in 1957. Portraits of the iguana, the giant tortoise, and these handsome sea lions or *Lobos marinos* appear in this first set. The purpose of the unusual issue was to publicize both the islands themselves and the 125th anniversary of Ecuador's possession of them.

Some form of sea lion or fur seal appears on this Uruguayan issue of 1954 picturing Seal Island or *Isla de Lobos.* The lighthouse and other buildings in the background seem to suggest that the sea lion colony and the human inhabitants have learned to get along together.

There are thirty-one species of animals in this world that all together are called the pinnipeds, members of the order Pinnipedia—the seals, sea lions, and walruses. A scientist who has spent many, many years studying these interesting creatures, Mr. Victor Scheffer, estimates that in all the world there are between fifteen and twenty-five million of these animals left. There can be little doubt that there once were many, many more.

Somewhere in the dim, rather mysterious past, probably during that period of time known as the Eocene (a period beginning about sixty million years ago, which ran for twenty or thirty million years), a strange and still unknown meat-eating mammal with legs began the return to the sea. No one knows what that animal looked like or just how or why he returned to the sea, but there, where competition was light, he began a new line of evolution that resulted in all the seals, sea lions, and walruses of today.

Most of the pinnipeds are clumsy on land but are streamlined for fast action in and under the waves. Even the great walruses and elephant seals are surprisingly agile once off land and in their natural element. Being mammals, the pinnipeds must come up for air and can't stay down as long as the whales, who are much larger. The pinnipeds have an advantage the whales don't have, however; they can come out of the water onto the land when they wish.

Pinnipeds vary greatly in size. The smallest is the ringed seal; a full-grown male will be under five feet long and will weigh under 200 pounds. The largest pinniped is the mammouth southern elephant seal. A large bull can be nearly twenty-two feet long and can weigh an amazing 8,000 pounds.

Pinnipeds vary greatly in number, as well. There may be as many as 5,000,000 ringed seals left, while the Caribbean monk seals are probably down to a dozen or so animals, and even they may be gone by the time you read these pages. Unless man is very careful, a number of species of the wonderful pinnipeds will vanish before our very eyes.

The seals and their relatives live mainly on fish. Some eat crabs, squid, and other delicacies from the sea, but it is safe to say that fish is the staple food. (The walruses prefer clams, and it is believed by some people that they dredge them out of the bottom with their great tusks.) Although the pinnipeds have no shortage of teeth (some have as many as thirty-eight), their mouths aren't made for biting things in half. They either swallow their meal whole or shake it apart with violent nods and gyrations of the head and neck.

Most of the seals, sea lions, and walruses are not overly friendly, and they are far more fun to watch than to play with. This is not to suggest that the pinnipeds of the world go around looking for trouble with man, but it is true that most pinnipeds can give a good nip when they set their minds to it. Generally, though, when you see the seals and their kin in the wild state, you will see some of nature's most joyful creations as they bob and dive and play endlessly in the sea.

The Jaguar (*Panthera onca*)

Mighty Spotted Cat of the New World

This superb Venezuelan airmail stamp of 1963 portrays the magnificent jaguar in his natural setting and in all his natural beauty. For its fine design and for its amazingly lifelike qualities, this stamp is one of my favorites. You will notice that the word *Felis* is used on this stamp, but *Panthera* is now preferred to *Felis* in the scientific name.

This Costa Rican airmail stamp of 1963 also pictures the jaguar but in a somewhat less lifelike pose. It is interesting to compare the way the same animal is treated on two different stamps. It should also be noted that this stamp, like the airmail from Venezuela, gives both a common and a scientific name for the animal pictured. This is becoming common practice around the world, probably out of respect for the topical collector who can go both blind and mad trying to identify animals.

It seems as if every South American country wants to show off as the home of the mighty jaguar. This 1960 stamp from Ecuador shows a fierce-looking specimen. Come to think of it, the jaguar is worth bragging about.

Paraguay wanted to show its jaguar, too. This 1969 painting of the mighty cat shows its strength. You can see the thick legs and the broad chest that make this animal so powerful. You can also see the jaguar's characteristic white belly.

The jaguar has been called the "leopard of South America," and while that is not exactly accurate, it is not very wrong either. Leopards come from Africa and Asia, while jaguars come from South America, Central America, and, rarely, from North America. The leopard is an old world cat, the jaguar a new world cat. The jaguar and the leopard probably had a common ancestor not so very long ago, but we do not know much about that at the moment.

The jaguar has his spots enclosed in dark rosettes and is a very beautiful animal from any point of view. Like the leopard, he is often found in the black or melano stage. Actually, if you look at a black jaguar very closely, you will see his spots, particularly if the rays of the sun are slanting at a shallow angle.

As the jaguar is beautiful, so is he powerful. He is a mighty hunter who is at home in the deep tropical jungle, on the high, open grass pampas, and even in the dry southwest of the United States. He occasionally turns up in Texas and Arizona after wandering northward from Mexico by following some of the heavily overgrown rivers that meander across the border. He is one of the best climbers in the world of cats, and a full-grown jaguar can run up a tree as well as you can run along a footpath. His powerful legs, haunches, and shoulders make him a mighty jumper, too, and he is able to go from a dead standstill to thirty or more miles an hour in a few seconds. All in all, the jaguar is rather like a coiled spring. One must be careful in dealing with him that the spring is not cut loose at the wrong time.

As always with any wonderfully dramatic-looking animal, there are a thousand tales of jaguars hunting men and doing great damage before being killed by the stout-hearted professional hunter who always shows up in time. While a jaguar certainly could make short work of an unarmed man and while it is probably quite true that an occasional jaguar goes bad and becomes a man-killer, most jaguars are quite content to mind their own business and leave man alone.

With so much of the wildlife in Africa killed off, many hunters are turning their eyes to the great jungles and forests of Central and South America. It is very much to be feared that the jaguar is in for a bad time in the years ahead. The forests of the great South American continent are so vast, however, that many will probably survive to save the species. In the years ahead, they will become increasingly difficult to see in the wild state, but it has never been an easy task because the jaguar is a very sly animal.

Like most cats the jaguar hasn't got a very good sense of smell. His eyes and his ears, though, are amazingly sharp, and he can follow his prey, or his enemy, for mile after mile in the thickest jungle by sound alone. Many a jaguar hunter who has thought that he was trailing a cat awoke to find that all the time the cat was trailing him!

The jaguar is beautiful and powerful. He is also one of the great meat-eaters left on our planet and a living symbol of the *wild* in *wild*life. Long may his rosetted spots grace the natural wonder of the natural world!

The Moose *(Alces alces)*

Lordly Deer of the North

In 1957 Russia issued a wildlife set portraying a deer, partridge, polar bear, bison, wild duck, moose, and sable; in 1959–60 the hare, Siberian horse, tiger, squirrel, marten, pheasant, and swan were added; and in 1961, the bear, beaver, and another deer were pictured. The moose shown here is not very good by the usual Russian stamp standards. Although technically the position of the animal is probably acceptable, he somehow doesn't look quite right.

In 1964 Russia issued another wildlife collection. The moose this time, although less "realistic," somehow seems more natural. Although this is an apparent contradiction, it somehow seems that the later moose is truer to form and mood.

The head of a moose appears on this good-looking 1967–1968 Swedish stamp—part of a wildlife series. Animals are often featured on Swedish stamps, and the renderings, as in this case, are frequently excellent.

The giant *Megaceros eurycerus,* an extinct ancestor of today's moose, is shown as a skeleton and as a museum reconstruction in this 1966 Romanian stamp. Many prehistoric animals appear on stamps from a number of countries.

It was once thought that the moose was naturally subject to epilepsy and that when it was seized by a fit, it cured itself by rubbing its ear with its left hind foot until the blood flowed. For this reason the left hind foot of a moose was thought a sure cure for human epilepsy or "the falling sickness" when it was placed over the patient's heart. There were six or eight other diseases thought curable with this token of the moose, and many of these great animals, it must be feared, were killed quite foolishly.

Although he is about as good at curing human diseases as are most witches' brews, the moose *is* a very interesting fellow. Even though he is found in the United States, Canada, Norway, Sweden, Russia, Manchuria, Siberia, and all the way around the world in the great forests of the North, nobody would know what you were talking about if you called him a moose anyplace but in the United States and Canada. Everywhere else in the world, our moose is known as an elk. The animal we call elk is really a wapiti. It can get quite confusing!

Elk or moose, by whatever name, this animal is a very large deer. Adult bulls can weigh over a half a ton and stand nearly seven feet at the shoulder.

From the time he is a year old, the bull moose starts growing antlers each year. While they are only knobs the first year, by the time a moose is six years old he is often developing antlers of almost impossible sizes. By September of each year the moose has rubbed the velvet off his great weapons, and by February or March of the following year his antlers will be shed, and he will soon be ready to grow a new pair.

Each year when his great antlers are free of velvet and at their sharpest, the bulls fight for the cows. Their great battles, fought far from human sight or hearing, are sometimes so violent that the bulls get their antlers locked together and can't pull them apart. Both animals then die of starvation.

Except in the fall, when the bulls and the cows meet briefly, the moose is a solitary creature. He doesn't like the company of other animals, even other moose, and man least of all. His eyesight isn't terribly sharp, but his hearing and sense of smell appear to be good. Only in the fall, during the breeding season, will the bulls look for trouble. The cows, however, can be dangerous when they are with their calves.

Despite his great size, the moose is fast and agile and almost completely fearless. He is a powerful swimmer and will not hesitate to swim a lake many miles across. He wanders through his private feeding range eating shrubs, bark, grass and various grasslike plants, weeds, and—his favorite of all—underwater plants. If left alone, the moose, however grumpy he may seem, will return the courtesy in a noble, gentlemanly way.

There were once many more moose than there are now, and they were found in many more states and provinces. Hunting is now restricted, and the moose that are left will almost certainly be able to keep their kind going for many more generations.

The Elephant (*Elephas* and *Loxodonta*)

Our Greatest Land Animal

The elephant is one of the most commonly pictured wild animals in the world of stamps. This handsome African elephant looks alert and ready for trouble. The stamp was issued by Angola, a Portuguese province on the southwest coast of Africa, in 1953 as part of a great animal set, one of the best ever issued. The other animals in the set are the leopard, sable, antelope, eland, crocodile, impala, zebra, sitatunga, rhinoceros, gemsbok, lion, buffalo, gazelle, gnu, jungle cow, wart hog, waterbuck, hippopotamus, greater kudu, and giraffe.

One of the stamps from the 1964 Russian wildlife set is this study of an Indian elephant. The loose-fitting skin characteristic of older animals can readily be seen in this almost humorous study.

In a 1963 wildlife set from India, this small-tusked bull is shown at a water hole. It is not easy to tell how very different the Indian elephant is from the African because of the angle chosen in this study.

The birds, insects, flowers, reptiles, and mammals of the former West African colony of Spanish Guinea (now Equatorial Guinea) were forever appearing on the colony's stamps. This triumphant-looking beast appeared in 1957 and is one of the most active of the many, many stamp-depicted elephants.

Just about everybody knows what an elephant looks like, and just about everybody knows a lot about these great beasts, the largest land animals left on earth. What many people don't realize is that much of what they know is nonsense.

Elephants live to be over a hundred years old! Remember hearing that? It isn't true, at least no more often than it is true of man. A seventy-year-old elephant is an old elephant indeed.

When elephants are about to die, they go to a secret valley that is full of tons and tons of valuable ivory! Remember that one? It isn't true. People with hotels and restaurants in elephant country like the idea, however, because a lot of people go there every year to look for this great graveyard.

Elephants never forget! Surely you recall hearing that. Well, they do have very impressive memories, but *never* is rather a long time. Very old elephants are probably quite forgetful.

Surely you have heard of elephants charging. Do you remember hearing about their running or galloping? No elephant ever ran, galloped, or did anything else but walk. An elephant can only walk, very fast indeed, but only walk. The biggest elephant in the world can't jump one foot. He can swim very well and can walk faster by far than the average man can run, but tricks like running and jumping are for animals with an altogether different kind of bone and muscle combination.

The Indian elephant and the African may be hard to separate in your mind, but if you ever saw the two side by side, you would see immediately how very different they really are. There are two kinds of elephants in Africa, the bush and the forest. The forest is the very much bigger of the two, and he is considerably larger than the Indian or Asiatic elephant. The ears on the African elephants are very, very much bigger than those on the Asiatic. The African elephant has a neck that appears to be very short, and his head does not rise much above the level of his back. Altogether he has a rather sloping look up front. The Asiatic elephant has two large knobs or bumps on the top of his head, and his neck appears to be rather longer. There are dozens of other differences as well, but those mentioned here will be immediately apparent.

Elephants are good family animals. They travel in herds, mind their own business, and take very good care of their young. Elephants appear to be extremely bright and have very large brains. They are so strong that it is almost impossible to believe some of the things they can do. Absolutely immense trees are pushed over by even an average-sized elephant if the leaves at the top look particularly tempting.

Although elephants are usually rather even-tempered animals, they can be provoked by anyone coming near their young. From time to time an elephant baby belonging to a careless mother will be killed by a lion in Africa or a tiger in India, but, generally speaking, the elephant has no real natural enemies except man.

The Tiger *(Panthera tigris)*

Great Striped Cat of Asia

Hungary's Budapest Zoo set of 1961 included portraits of a kangaroo, bison, brown bear, elephant, ibex, polar bear, zebra, bison cow with calf, and this tiger with her cubs. It was, and is, a particularly interesting set.

This dramatic study of a large tiger obviously very much on the alert is part of the 1963 fauna set from India. The fauna of a country is collectively all the animals that live there. The flora is the land's plant life. Another way of saying you collect animal stamps is to say you collect fauna stamps. It is a good scientific word.

This 1959–1960 Russian issue pictures a Siberian tiger in the snow. It is now believed that the great striped cat originally came from the North.

This 1964 Russian issue picturing a tiger is more stylized than the earlier issue but, somehow, not that much less realistic. The animal pictured is still very much a powerful tiger.

VANISHING ANIMAL

How great, how grand the striped cat of Asia! No animal exists that is more legitimately the living symbol of the world of wildlife. The tiger, much more than the lion, is king of the jungle. A migrant from the North, he is still to be found in Siberia, where the snow lies deep and the winters are long and cruel. In many parts of his range, notably in Bali and in Java, the tiger is becoming very scarce and will soon disappear unless hunting is prohibited.

The great tiger is, of course, an eater of meat, and meat is the only food he can live on. He is a powerful hunter able to kill every animal within his range except adult Asiatic elephants.

Tigers are generally very gentlemanly in their ways. They seldom kill more than they need for food and spend most of their time in quiet solitude. They do not travel in family groups like lions, but the mothers are excellent parents.

There have been many hair-raising tales about man-eating tigers, and legends have built up through the years. There have been times when old, crippled tigers, unable to hunt their normal fleet-footed prey, have turned to man-eating. Very often it has been found that such cats have been victimized by porcupines they themselves tried to kill. Porcupine quills in a paw or in the mouth and nose can put any tiger out of business. Man-eaters are terrible scourges when they occur, but fortunately most tigers are content to leave man alone.

The tiger is actually rather closely related to the lion. If you took a full-grown lion and a full-grown tiger and skinned them, it would take a real expert to tell their bones and muscles apart. The very apparent differences between the two cats are skin deep!

Tigers hunt more by stealth than lions do since they live in thicker forests and can be found in true jungle. They do not mind water at all and on a hot day will go for a swim just to cool off. When the weather is cold, however, they don't even like to get their feet wet. The tiger's hunting is helped by his keen eyesight, particularly sensitive to movement, and his very alert hearing. His sense of smell, though, like that of most cats, isn't very good.

The very brightly colored coat of the tiger would seem to be too wild to be of much use as camouflage but, in reality, serves very well to break up the tiger's outline as he stands in deep grass or thick jungle growth. He will often lie up very near to where domestic animals are being grazed and watch them carefully throughout the hot midday hours. When evening comes and the air cools, he moves down and makes his kill. Unless the animals scent him or unless the herdsman is particularly keen, he will not be detected until too late. When he takes to stock-raiding, he becomes a real menace, and the government usually steps in and helps hunt him down.

The Hippopotamus *(Hippopotamus* and *Choeropsis)*

With Grace and Particular Charm

In 1937, Liberia, a nation of 43,000 square miles on the west coast of Africa, issued a triangular wildlife set. Included were an elate hornbill, a harnessed antelope, a West African dwarf buffalo, a great white egret, and this pygmy hippopotamus. It is a very desirable set as the animals are well represented by their portraits.

French West Africa, which has since been divided into many independent nations, put the hippopotamus and the crocodile together for this dual portrait in 1947. The old hippo seems upset about something.

The well-known wildlife set from the Mozambique Company (issue of 1937) contained this study of two hippopotamuses partially submerged. This is a particularly realistic study.

The South African wildlife set of 1954 included a wart hog, rhinoceros, lion, gnu, leopard, zebra, elephant, kudu, springbok, gemsbok, nyala, giraffe, sable antelope, and this old hippo calling his challenge to the world. Since stamps travel all around the world as ambassadors and since tourism inspired by wildlife is a major industry in many parts of Africa, African stamps have often pictured wildlife. It seems quite natural that animals appear more often on stamps from the nations of Africa than from any other continent on earth.

(for pygmy hippopotamus only) VANISHING ANIMAL

There are actually two kinds or species of hippopotamuses left on earth, although once there were more. The "big" hippopotamus (whose scientific name is *Hippopotamus amphibius*) was once found throughout most of Africa in all rivers and streams with deep water. There are now few if any in the northern parts of the continent. Man and his weapons have pushed the great beasts to the southern parts. The "big" hippo is a creature of lakes, rivers, and streams and is happiest when his watery world borders on some good marshes and reed beds. He is not a very friendly creature, and the mighty bulls fight among themselves constantly. You rarely see a bull without great scars. They use their enormous lower tusks to damage each other, often severely.

The second kind of hippopotamus, the pygmy, is found only in western Africa, the Ivory Coast, Liberia, and Sierra Leone. He is more an animal of the damp forests and swamps than the lakes and rivers.

Though this ungainly giant of Africa is considered aquatic, this applies more to the big hippopotamus than the pygmy. The big hippopotamus spends most of his day wholly or partially submerged and rarely comes out onto dry land until the late afternoon or evening. If you frighten a big hippopotamus, you will invariably see him dash into the water and submerge. If you startle a pygmy hippo, he will crash off into the forest.

The baby hippos, however, are actually born under water, and they nurse under water. It is true that they can swim before they can walk. The mother hippopotamus makes a very good parent and takes great pains to protect her baby against large cats on land and the ever present crocodile in the water. The baby often scrambles up on its mother's back to sun itself while she is submerged. That probably affords some protection against marauding crocodiles.

Both species of hippopotamus are strictly vegetarians. Despite their fierce-looking teeth and their great mouths, they eat only grasses, reeds, and other land and water plants. Sometimes they enter cultivated fields to dine on the fruit of man's labor, and the damage they can do in one night is truly awe-inspiring. Too many visits by a herd of hippos could make any farmer overlook the conservation laws. Hippos are being thinned out rather too rapidly in some areas. In the years ahead the problem will become more acute.

Both species have special pores in their sparsely haired skin that secrete a pinkish oil sometimes called "blood sweat." It is thick and greasy and protects the animal whether it is in the water or out in dry air.

An adult of the "big" species can weigh as much as five tons. An adult of the pygmy species will weigh as much as five hundred pounds, but seldom very much more. Both species can live as long as thirty-five or forty years. They are seldom troubled by anything but man once they achieve adult size.

The Galago (*Galago senegalensis* and others)

Cousin to the Monkey

A 1959 extremely colorful wildlife set from what was formerly the Belgian Congo included this fetching portrait of the galago. It is a good example of a small and unusual mammal appearing on a stamp. Not just elephants, lions, and the other obvious species appear on the stamps of the world, although they do appear more often!

The bush-baby or galago showed up on this 1966 stamp from Kenya—part of a fauna set. These animals are so shy and secretive that you would be more apt to see one on a stamp than in the flesh, even if you were in Kenya.

Fernando Po, formerly a province of Spain and now part of the independent nation of Equatorial Guinea, is an island in the Gulf of Guinea off the west coast of Africa. In this 1967 stamp picturing a galago, notice the characteristic startled look in the eyes.

Some people have confused the loris with the galago. They are related—that is obvious—but they are quite different animals. The galago is from Africa, the loris from Asia. A slender loris for you to compare with our galago appears on this 1970 stamp from Ceylon. Ceylon, an island in the Indian Ocean, is now known as Sri Lanka.

The galago is a small relative of the monkey and therefore of man and the great apes. He is what is known as a *primate*, and so are you!

Although not all scientists agree by any means, the galago is generally lumped together in one family (the *Lorisidae*) with the lorises, the pottos, the bush babies, the angwantibos, and the nagapies. You say that you don't recognize these animals? That is the fun and interest of collecting stamps in this way—you meet such interesting creatures. Let's get familiar with this one member of the loris family, at least, the soft, cuddly-looking, big-eyed galago.

He is found, generally, in the bush and forest regions of Africa south of the great, burning Sahara Desert. He is found, as well, on some of the islands off the coast, like Zanzibar.

During the day the galago sleeps in masses of extremely dense vegetation, hiding from sunlight and his enemies. He is active only at night and then usually confines his activity to the world of the tall tree. He is what we call *arboreal*. He likes to stay close to others of his kind, particularly during the day. Several will curl up together in an old bird nest, tree fork, or some other suitable bedding site.

When the galago is alert, always after dark, he is swift and agile, making great leaps from tree to tree. If awakened during the day, he can barely stumble around. On those rare occasions when he is on the ground, he hops along on his hind legs like a kangaroo.

Galagos (and all their relatives) use their hands very, very well. They defend themselves, hunt, grasp, and pick up articles. Their long fingers and toes have flattened nails. Their favorite food is the grasshopper, but they also seem to enjoy birds' eggs, birds, fruit, and various seeds and flowers. They are busy little creatures in their nighttime world of the treetops, and they build up a really healthy appetite.

The mother galago will bear one or two young at a time. It takes her about 110 days to produce them. Before her babies arrive, the galago mother uses her dexterous little hands to build a nest for them. After they are born, they ride around with their mother by clinging tightly to her fur. Within a couple of weeks of their birth, the babies can walk and even make short leaps. It is three and a half months or more, however, before they can get along without their mother's milk. It has been said that the galago can live as long as ten years.

No matter what you call him, galago, bush-baby, ojam, changa, komba, kideri, or kashila, this little primitive primate is one of the most delightful creatures hiding in nature's secret places. Because he is a nighttime creature and because he doesn't destroy the crops or the works of man, no one bothers very much with him. He will probably survive for as long as man doesn't destroy too much of his natural habitat.

The Manatee and the Dugong (*Dugong* and *Hydrodamalis*)

The Ugly Mermaids

This attractive triangle from Costa Rica pictures a rather jolly-looking manatee. The year of issue was 1963. Costa Rica is situated in Central America between Nicaragua and Panama. Its total area is almost 20,000 square miles, and its capital is San José.

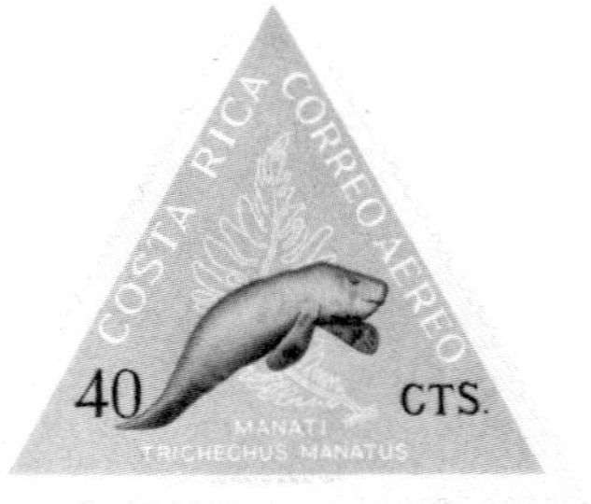

The Republic of the Niger was formerly a French colony. It is in northern Africa, directly north of Nigeria. This 1962 issue pictures the manatee or *mantin*. It was issued to call attention to the very important *protection de la faune*.

The United Republic of Cameroon gave its manatee a nursing baby, emphasizing that this animal is a mammal. This is a pleasing stamp with the mother manatee looking very real and very natural. It appeared in 1962.

The Ryukyus, an island group that is part of Japan, featured a dugong on this 1966 stamp. How do we tell this is a dugong and not a manatee? Look at the tail and compare it with the other stamps shown in this chapter. Besides, manatees don't come from that part of the world.

One of the smallest orders of mammals in the world is the order Sirenia, the dugongs, sea cows, and manatees. There is one dugong, found from the east coast of Africa eastward to the Philippines and Australia, one sea cow that is probably extinct, and three manatees, one from the United States, one from South America, and one from western Africa. For the whole world, that is all the Sirenia there are.

The Sirenia are animals that have returned to the water for good. They are like the whales in that they have no choice at all. Dry land is not for them. The seals, at least, have a choice.

Steller's sea cow, a great lumbering creature weighing as much as four to five tons and measuring up to twenty-five feet in length, wasn't even discovered until 1742. It was confined to the waters around Bering Island and a few other small islands of the Komandorskie group in the Bering Sea. As soon as they were discovered, man began to hunt them, and it took just twenty-seven years to kill off all the known specimens. Now there are reports from time to time that seem to indicate that some may still survive in the chilly, fog-shrouded waters of the Bering Sea. If they are rediscovered, it will be an exciting day for natural history!

The dugong is a tropical warm-water animal that seldom ventures far asea or far into fresh water. He likes quiet coastal areas with as little human traffic as possible. He is a peaceful creature and doesn't bother anybody or anything. He feeds on marine algae and grasses that grow along the coast in shallow water. He can stay submerged for as long as ten minutes, but, like all mammals, must come up for air.

The manatees are warm-water creatures like their cousin the dugong. They gather in small groups in salt, brackish, and fresh water to eat the plant life that grows submerged or hangs down over the water from the banks. They will swim far upstream and live very well quite far from the sea as long as the weather doesn't turn cold. If it drops below forty, they may die.

The manatee's upper lip is quite unusual. It is split in two, and each side can work independently of the other, rather like a pair of forceps. The stout bristles on the manatee's snout also help direct food into the mouth. One manatee can easily pack away as much as ninety to a hundred pounds of food in a day. A full-grown manatee may weigh close to nine hundred pounds and can be more than a dozen feet long. They are dull gray all over, have tiny eyes, and no external ears. They are not a very fetching-looking group of animals.

Unfortunately, the manatee has fine-tasting meat, a good, useful hide, and a high-quality oil. He has been hunted for these reasons and today is found in very reduced numbers. Hunting is now forbidden in the United States, and Florida will fine anyone caught killing one as much as $500. Maybe the manatee will survive man after all!

The Zebra (*Equus* sp.)

The Little Striped Cousin to the Horse

The South African wildlife set of 1954 included this portrait of a zebra. The zebra has been a favorite on the stamps of many African countries down through the years. There have been many handsome studies, and some of the issues are now quite rare.

The set from the Mozambique Company in 1937 included a number of fine animal studies, including this striking zebra. He appears to be very alert in this portrait.

Two zebras are shown on this 1971 stamp from the Somali Democratic Republic. The stamp is part of a set featuring African wildlife. It was issued, no doubt, to attract tourists since stamps are a good form of advertising.

Poland often features wildlife from all over the world. This very handsome stamp of 1972, showing a fine zebra, is especially good.

All of the horses and horselike animals of the world belong to the one family Equidae. The most colorful of these, and the best known wild members of family by far, are the zebras. They are found in the part of Africa that is south of the fierce Sahara Desert. They are happiest, generally, on the plains and savannas, although some are found in mountainous areas at rather surprising altitudes.

The zebra doesn't like to be alone. He is usually found in herds of his own kind, but if separated from his family, he will readily join up with herds of other animals, even flocks of ostriches. There is nothing snobby about a zebra.

Although a zebra can run as fast as forty miles an hour, he is easily killed. He has one very bad shortcoming, his curiosity. He can't resist investigating something new and exciting and so is an easy mark for any hunter. He is one of the lion's favorite foods, and the leopard doesn't turn his nose up at zebra steak either.

The herds of zebra that once ranged over the African savanna were seemingly without end. Surely, they numbered in the many millions of animals. There were so many, in fact, that no one could have believed anything could happen to threaten their survival. Before 1860, however, the Quagga, a strange-looking zebra with pale stripes, had disappeared from the wild. The last one died in a zoo in Holland in 1883, a sad last survivor of an exciting race of wild animals.

The zebras that remain in Africa may survive if man will observe his own laws and stop poaching. This is unlikely to happen, however, and the zebra may one day be in very serious difficulty.

Zebras are resistant to many African diseases that have proven to be disastrous for horses. It has therefore been thought a very good idea to crossbreed horses and zebras to take advantage of this resistance. So far the results have not been good. There are zebra-horse and zebra-ass combinations to be seen but not enough to make the experiments very successful or even significant.

Zebras themselves don't tame very easily, and in plain fact zebras tend to be rather high-strung, even nasty critters, not at all the sort you would want around your farmyard no matter how colorful their coat.

A full-grown zebra can weigh as much as 750 pounds and stand almost five feet at the shoulder, although that is a little on the large size for most zebras you are apt to see. They breed very well in captivity and are one of the most commonly seen animals in zoos around the world. Some circus trainers have had a measure of luck in getting them to perform, but it takes a lot of work. A zebra who doesn't like performing doesn't need lessons in self-expression; an unhappy zebra kicks and bites most professionally.

Someone once described a zebra as a horse with fancy pajamas on. That may be suitable enough, but the zebra is much, much more. He is a flash of light on an open plain; he is natural art in the sun. Beautiful, graceful, frequently playful, sociable, swift, and alive, the zebra is one of the great and wonderful sights of the natural world.

The Leopard *(Panthera pardus)*

Spotted Cat of Africa and Asia

The South African wildlife set of 1954 that we have referred to so often in this book included this profile of the leopard, mighty hunter of the night.

Nyasaland, formerly a British protectorate of over 37,000 square miles on Lake Nyasa in southeast Africa, coupled a rather strange "long" leopard and King George VI on this 1938–1944 issue. Nyasaland is now an independent nation called Malawi.

The leopard stands in angry defiance on this stamp from Angola's 1953 wildlife set. Whoever the intruder was in this study, he was resented mightily.

One of the more dramatic portraits of the leopard appeared on this 1942 stamp from the former Belgian Congo.

The leopard is one of the truly great predators of the world. He is found throughout Africa south of the Sahara Desert and may still be found in many parts of Asia. He ranges from tropical forests to rocky areas with a variety of cover to the frigid arctic conditions of the high Himalayas.

The leopard we are discussing here should not be confused with the magnificent clouded leopard, for they are two very different cats. The clouded leopard, or pungmar, is found in Nepal and Sikkim, in China, Formosa, Sumatra, Borneo, and parts of Malaysia. He has great blotches and not spots.

The snow leopard, or ounce, is also a very different creature and one some people think the most beautiful of all. He is found in the highlands of central Asia and is not a jungle or forest animal at all. He is at home above the tree line.

The common leopard, African leopard, or Indian leopard—whatever you choose to call him—is closely related to the lion, the tiger, and the jaguar. He is the smallest of all these but by no means the least to be reckoned with. He is a powerful hunter and can carry kills much larger than himself up a tree with very little effort.

Although there is endless confusion on the subject, there is no difference between a spotted leopard and a black panther except their fur color. Two spotted leopards can have a black panther for a cub, and two black panthers can beget a spotted leopard. The two different color *phases* can be litter mates, brothers and sisters. It is just that the leopard tends toward *melanism*, or very dark colors. In the right light, you can see that the black panther has spots, too.

The lion and the tiger tend to be rather calm animals unless things go very wrong. Even the jaguar, with his oversized curiosity, is rather easy-going most of the time. The leopard is not so disposed. He is excitable, even hysterical, a good part of the time. He is very quick to anger, very quick to attack. He is often in trouble because of it.

The leopard likes dogs very much, not as friends but to eat. He will wander into a native village at night to look for a tasty dog, and if he encounters a man or woman out wandering, he is apt to get so excited that he will attack. Men and women injured in this way often suffer terrible mutilation, and the leopard has to be hunted as a man-killer. Unfortunately, leopards become actual man-eaters from time to time and present a terrible problem until they are tracked down and killed. Man-eating leopards, while not common, are very brazen and very dangerous.

The leopard prefers to hunt by night but will be about during the daylight hours if he is hungry enough. He loves baboons and is that animal's worst enemy. Any leopard about will set off a tribe of baboons into the worst kind of screaming and scolding. Unhappily, a great many animals feel the same way about the leopard.

The leopard's one great fault is that he has a big appetite. He is really not at all "blood-thirsty" or "vicious." He only knows to kill when he is hungry, just as he seeks water when he is thirsty and some secluded spot when he is tired. Tired, hungry, or thirsty, the leopard is one of the most handsome animals in the whole world.

The Whale (Cetacea)

The Biggest Animal That Ever Lived

This 1963 issue from Russia shows a whale factory ship, a whale killer ship, and a baleen whale in Antarctic waters.

This 1961 issue from Bulgaria pictures a pair of common dolphins leaping in their characteristic graceful arc. These playful animals can cavort like this for hours at a time. Dolphins, of course, are just a species of small whale.

This 1957 semipostal stamp from the Netherlands pictures a great baleen whale and the ship *Willem Barendsz.* A semipostal is a stamp issued by a country's government to raise money for a special cause.

This 1960 semipostal from Fernando Po shows natives in a small open boat harpooning a great baleen whale. It is very dangerous work and always has been!

(for large whales only) VANISHING ANIMAL

If you took a hundred people and stood them with their backs to the rail of a ship and said, "There's a whale!" how many do you think would turn around to look? Probably all one hundred. Whales fascinate everyone, for they are not only the largest animals that ever lived on this planet, but also some of the strangest left on earth.

Whales are mammals just as squirrels, pigs, monkeys, and human beings are. They require air, they give birth to living young, and they feed their babies with mother's milk. Somehow it is exciting to look at a creature like a blue or sulphur-bottom whale that is 100 feet long and probably weighs 130 tons and realize that whales and men are both part of the wonderful world of mammals.

There are basically two kinds of whales—the toothed whales and the baleen whales. The largest toothed whale is the sperm whale. The sperm loves squid particularly, and in the great depths of the sea, down where the sun never shines, the forty- to sixty-foot sperm whale attacks squid as long as himself. Here, in the mysterious realm so foreign to man, some of the world's greatest animal contests are waged. The sperm whale, we believe, always wins, or at least almost always. He can be badly scarred in the process, however, for the squid can give a good account of itself.

The great baleen whales, the largest whales of all, have given up teeth for baleen plates that look like vast, hairy venetian blinds running up and down in their mouths. These hairy plates are giant strainers, for the biggest whales eat the smallest food. These giants move through seemingly endless fields of plankton, extremely small marine life, and filter out tons of food. In the Antarctic, where the greatest concentrations of really big whales are still to be found, they filter out billions of small red shrimp called krill. How many tiny red shrimp does it take to feed a whale that weighs a hundred tons? That is almost like asking, "How high is up?"

The porpoises and dolphins that so many sea-goers see playing around the bow of their ship every year are small whales, too, all part of a group of animals called *Cetacea*. They are all descended from land animals that a very, very long time ago returned to an easy life in the sea. Unless whaling ships are around, life is easy in the sea for the whales, for there is seldom a food shortage.

Whales are often found washed up on the beach, although no one knows why they come there and get trapped. A whale on dry land must soon die of suffocation. He has lived in the world of water for so long that he has lost the muscles necessary to keep heaving his great bulk up enough to allow his lungs to fill. He soon tires of the unnatural task and perishes.

Whaling down through the years has pushed many species to the danger point, and unless very careful steps are taken, some species will become extinct in our lifetime.

The Hyena (*Hyaena* and *Crocuta*)

The Misunderstood

Mauritania, now a republic, was formerly a French colony in northwestern Africa bordering on the Atlantic Ocean. Its area is over 415,000 square miles; its capital, once known as St. Louis, is now Nouakchott. This 1963 issue shows the spotted hyena found in many parts of Africa.

Since Fujairah has a population of only 7,000 people, you might wonder why they issue so many stamps. I guess it is the only way they can tell anybody that they are there! The hyenas on this 1969 issue look particularly evil. Stamps made solely for collectors are often overdone!

This airmail stamp from Iraq (issued in 1969) features the striped hyena. The profile view shows the sloping back and weak hindquarters that are so characteristic of this interesting animal. I wonder why the artist felt he had to show the jaws open and the muzzle slightly back. Perhaps he felt people wouldn't believe it was a hyena unless he made it look fierce.

Dahomey gave their spotted hyena a bunch of bones to make him look nasty and catch people's fancy. Actually, though, the animal itself is rather well done on this stamp. The head seems just right. The year was 1969.

Just why it is that some groups of animals get bad reputations—generally much worse than they deserve—is not easy to determine. Such is the case with the hyena.

There is a small group of meat-eating mammals or carnivores known as the *Hyaenidae*. The family consists of a strange African creature, the aardwolf (which is, of course, not a real wolf at all), the spotted or laughing hyena from Africa, the striped hyena from India and other parts of Asia, and the brown hyena from Africa. Although the family is small, it is an interesting one.

The nearest relatives of the hyenas are probably a group of animals known as the viverine—the mongooses, the genet, and the civets. They are all quite respectable in age, going far back in the history of mammals.

The spotted or laughing hyena is the largest and most aggressive member of the family. A big male can be over three feet high at the shoulder and weigh close to 200 pounds. They den in dense vegetation or a cave, if either is available, or in a hole in the ground if that is the best they can do. While all hyenas are very important to nature because they help clean up the carrion, the spotted hyena does not limit himself to the leavings of other predators. He will make his own kills—including sheep, goats, and calves—and will even take human children and sleeping adults. Some become regular man-eaters. Spotted hyenas tend to be rather cowardly (although that is again a word for humans more than animals) and appear unwilling to stick to prey that puts up a good, stiff fight unless there are several of them hunting together. Their jaws are immensely powerful, and they can crush the heaviest of bones. Their call sounds rather like an insane laugh, and it is an eerie sound in the night.

The brown and the striped hyena (from Africa and Asia, respectively) are much smaller beasts and seldom weigh more than 120 pounds. Like their spotted cousin they have coarse hair and a not-too-pleasant odor. The hair along their spines can be a foot long.

The brown and striped hyenas eat carrion for the most part. They do kill some animals when they have the opportunity, however. They are most active at night and are not as noisy as their larger cousin. They make a great show of anger when attacked but seldom put up much of a fight.

Some African natives take advantage of the hyenas' taste for carrion and waste. They leave all their domestic refuse out for them at night. Nothing is left in the morning.

The funny-looking aardwolf, while related to the hyenas, has adopted quite a different diet. He eats termites and the grubs of insects he digs out of the ground. He lives in great holes dug in the ground and is neither aggressive nor troublesome. He is becoming quite rare and must be protected or he will soon vanish forever from the face of the earth.

Not handsome, brave, or attractive in their habits, the hyenas have become symbols of "low-life" in the natural world, but they are just as interesting in their ways as any other group of animals.

The Panda *(Ailuropeda melanoleuca)*

Symbol for All

In all the world there are only two species of panda, and both appear on stamps. On this 1963 stamp from India is the Himalayan or lesser panda in a characteristic pose.

The 1964 wildlife set from Russia includes this giant panda or Pei-Hsiung. It is a particularly pleasing portrait.

In 1961 Belgium gave us the small red or lesser panda on this wildlife stamp. Belgium is a long way from panda country, but this head-on view is well done. It is so lifelike that it gives the feeling it is a retouched photograph and not a painting.

This 1969 stamp from the People's Republic of China offers a pleasing artist's rendition of the giant panda. The pose with the bamboo stalk is very natural. This is more painting than portrait, but it works very well. It "feels" like a giant panda as much as it looks like one.

Among the mammals of the world that eat meat at least part of the time is a particularly interesting group known as the Procyonidae. The family is made up of very different-looking members including the ring-tailed cats of Central and North America (which are not cats at all), the raccoon, the coatimundi, the kinkajou, and the world's only two pandas, the lesser and the giant.

The lesser panda has many different names. In various places he is called red panda, Himalayan panda, Himalayan raccoon, red cat-bear, wah, ye, and sankam. He is neither a bear, a cat, nor a raccoon, although he is related quite closely to the latter. The lesser panda, funny little creature that he is, is still found in several parts of China, Burma, Sikkim, and Nepal. He likes high elevations and doesn't seem to mind the cold at all, which is not true of his giant cousin.

The lesser panda is a gentle little creature that is both curious and tame in captivity, but he doesn't seem to live very long when removed from his native highlands. He seldom eats meat but prefers bamboo shoots, grass, roots, fruit, and some nuts. He occasionally eats birds' eggs, rarely, perhaps, a bird. His weight runs from six to ten pounds usually, and his total length, including that long, bushy tail, runs forty to forty-five inches.

His deep rusty color, his rounded head and alert ears, and his attractive face markings all combine to make a very pleasing-looking little animal. He doesn't bother anybody, doesn't destroy anything, and prefers the privacy of his quiet life. He sleeps in the trees during the day and feeds mostly at night. The lesser pandas travel in pairs or family groups and make very good parents.

The giant panda is very much larger than his lesser cousin. He can be as much as five and a half feet long and can weigh 350 pounds. His black and white markings are too well known by children everywhere to need describing here.

He is often called a panda bear, and although he may look a lot like a bear when you first see him, he really is much more closely related to the raccoon than to old bruin. The giant panda is found only in China, and we don't have any idea how many there are left in the world.

It takes a giant panda a whole day just to feed himself. For nearly twelve hours, 365 days of the year, he wanders around, usually all by himself, feeding on bamboo shoots and roots, on flowers like the iris and the crocus, on certain favored grasses, and even on fish and small rodents.

The panda cubs weigh about five pounds at birth, and you would never expect that they would multiply that weight by seventy by the time they reach full growth.

Pandas are favorite zoo animals, although they are not often seen now. They are very much like clowns when they are cubs and remain quite gentle when grown. When they became known to the world at large some years ago, they caught the imagination of children in almost every country and must be rated one of the most popular animals ever known.

The Camel (*Camelus*)

The Slave of Man

Just south of Egypt in northeastern Africa lies the Republic of the Sudan, nearly a million square miles of forbidding country. There the economy would perish without the camel. This 1954 issue shows a camel and rider.

A camel mother and calf appear in this charming portrait on a 1901 issue from Nyassa, when it was a part of Portuguese East Africa.

Spanish Sahara is a Spanish overseas province on the west coast of Africa, south of Morocco. A great many more stamps are issued by Spanish Sahara than the inhabitants, most of whom never write letters, could ever possibly use. They are issued to earn revenue from stamp collectors, and they frequently picture wildlife. These two dromedaries, on a stamp issued in 1957, seem to have created a forest of knobby knees.

Mauritania, in northwestern Africa, borders on the Atlantic Ocean. This rather fierce-looking gentleman perched on his camel first appeared in 1938.

(for bactrian only) VANISHING ANIMAL

The family of animals known as the Camelidae consists of the two different camels we will discuss in this chapter, plus the alpaca, the llama, the guanaco, and the vicuna. All but the true camels come from South America, where they are domesticated just as the camels are in their native lands.

The two-humped or bactrian camel comes from China, Turkistan, and Mongolia. He stands about six feet at the shoulder and weighs as much as three-quarters of a ton. Not quite so tall as his one-humped cousin, nor quite as speedy, he is more gentle and much easier to ride. His hair is used to make a good, heavy fabric, his meat is eaten with particular relish by some people, and his milk is given to human babies and is also used to make cheese and a kind of intoxicating drink.

The story that camels can store vast quantities of water in their stomachs is not true. They do not store very much at all, and although they can do better without water for longer periods of time than most animals, they certainly can't get on for very long. After a very few days they start to lose both weight and strength rapidly. If kept without adequate food for long, they become the victims of wilting humps. Their humps actually get soft and start to droop.

There are still some wild bactrian camels left in remote regions, and they are seen from time to time in small groups, but there are probably many more in captivity than in the wild.

The one-humped camel or dromedary is not a very pleasant fellow, and when he is in a particularly bad mood, he has the foul habit of spitting, often quite accurately, at the nearest human being. If the unfortunate victim is near enough, he is likely to be bitten as well.

There probably aren't any one-humped camels left in the wild except those that have escaped from careless owners. They *probably* came originally from Arabia, although that is not known for sure. They have been carted all over the world by now and are apt to turn up almost anywhere. They are now used in Australia and were once used in the American Southwest (where wonderful legends grew up around them) and in many other desert areas as well.

Despite their nasty manners, the one-humped camels make very efficient servants of man and good companions to have on a desert crossing. They will eat the worst imaginable kinds of plants, kinds that other animals couldn't possibly digest or thrive on. They will drink any kind of water, even salt water, will carry great loads over long distances, and will tolerate terrible weather. Throughout it all, they will grumble and complain bitterly, but if things get really bad, they can be eaten.

There is more to their name *ship of the desert* than may meet the eye. The name is meant to imply that they are used in commerce as carriers of cargo. Indeed that is so, but there is another way in which they resemble ships. They roll fiercely as they move along, and if you happen to be perched on top, it is quite possible to get really terribly seasick many, many miles from the nearest sea.

The Little Tiger Cat (Dasyuridae)

Rare Citizen of Australia

In 1959 Australia pictured the rare little tiger cat on this eight-penny stamp in a set that included the banded anteater, the kangaroo, the bandicoot, and the duck-billed platypus.

The tiger cat is another of those animals that may appear on stamps just once—although you never know, of course. Here are three more marsupials—distant relatives of the tiger cat—all from Papua New Guinea. They are the pen-tailed phalanger (*Distoechurus*), the phalanger, and the New Guinean possum (*Dactylonax*). A good part of the study of wildlife, of course, is making connections, determining how animals are related to each other and who descended from whom. The organization of a faunal stamp collection is no different—it only makes sense when it is in some kind of order that reflects the actual world of animals. These Papua New Guinea stamps, which appeared in 1971, are particularly fine—the portraits of the animals are excellent and the scientific names are shown. Without those names, identification of the animals could be impossible.

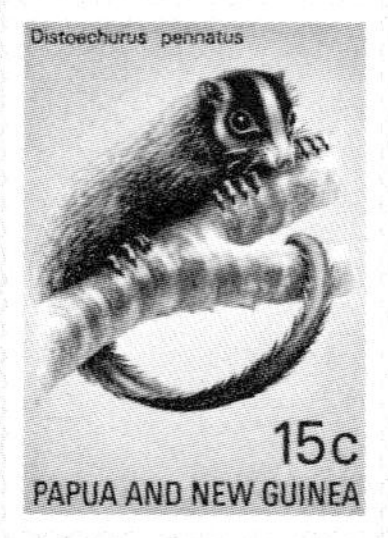

Among the strange and exotic animal life of Australia is this little inhabitant of the dense and tangled underbrush of eastern Australia and parts of Tasmania. The tiger cat does not appear outside of heavy forest country.

Even with his long, slightly bushy tail, the tiger cat is rarely more than four feet long and almost never weighs more than eight pounds. He is a rich brown on top and a pale sandy color underneath. His spots are generally white. He can be distinguished from similar animals by the fact that his spots extend down onto his tail. On the other animals, the spots do not.

If you encounter a tiger cat (who is not a tiger and not a cat) in the wild, you will be treated to a show of fierce temper. He will hiss, even scream, and give all the signs of a truly ferocious beast. The chances are, though, if you are quiet and don't rush matters, you can capture him without even being bitten.

The tiger cat is a meat-eater and is very swift in pursuit of his varied prey. He hunts mostly at night and mostly on the ground. He will dine happily on a wide selection of small mammals and birds, and even insects.

This strange little creature is a marsupial and gives birth to very underdeveloped young. They are kept in the mother's pouch just as kangaroos are. At birth the babies are less than one half an inch long. At the end of one month they have grown to nearly an inch and a half. At seven weeks they become detached from their mother's nipples, start to get fur, and begin to open their eyes. They grow rapidly after that.

The tiger cat is an active little animal and is ever anxious to be up and at the world. When clouds roll in and darken the daytime sky, he will not wait for night to come but will come down out of his tree, or out of his den, and have a go at the business of living. He is alert and often stops and sits up on his haunches to look around. He also uses that position to eat. His hands are very dexterous, and he can even capture prey by grasping them.

Nobody knows how many tiger cats there are in the world, but the remote forests of Australia and Tasmania will probably provide shelter for a good population for years to come. It is very important that the wildlife of Australia be preserved because that whole vast land provides a wonderful laboratory for scientists to study. In these strange animals from "down under" can be seen the ways in which animals evolve and adapt themselves to different environments and to different ways of life. There is no place quite like Australia anywhere else on our planet and no animals quite like its strange marsupials, including, of course, the tiger cat with the spots on his tail.

The Gaur (*Bos gaurus*)

Great Horned Creature of India

This 1963 wildlife stamp from India portrays in a particularly handsome manner the dramatic gaur. He looks as if he will come to life at any moment and come walking off the stamp.

The 1961 Hungarian set honoring the Budapest Zoo featured the gaur—showing a cow with her calf. It is a long way from Hungary to gaur country, but since they are found in zoos, this stamp from the middle of Europe makes sense. The animals aren't very well done, and the drama of the creature is lacking.

This stamp was issued in 1972 by the Khmer Republic—the official name for the country commonly called Cambodia. The Khmers were an ancient people of Cambodia whose language is still spoken there. The stamp is a dramatic but honest study and is very well done; the guar looks alert and powerful.

The animal kingdom can often be a rather confusing place, and when we come to the matter of cattle, it can be very mixed up. The cattle of the world belong to a family known as the Bovidae. This family includes the antelopes, the water buffaloes, the bison, the true cattle, the gazelles, the chamois, the goats, the musk oxen, the sheep, and a whole host of other varied creatures. There are about 115 different species in all.

The true cattle of the world probably number no more than seven species, although there were once many more. There has been so much crossbreeding in captivity that it is almost impossible to trace the line back to see where our "cows" and "bulls" come from. Their relatives in the wild today consist of the ankole cattle, which have been domesticated since before man began to write his own history; the zebu of India; the yak of China, Tibet, and India; the gayal of India, Assam, and Burma; the banteng, which is very, very rare in his native Southeast Asia; the kouprey of Indo-China or Cambodia; and the subject of this chapter, the handsome gaur.

The mighty gaur can stand close to seven feet at the shoulder and may weigh considerably more than a ton. During the last century he could still be found wild in India, Nepal, Assam, Burma, Cambodia, down the Malay Peninsula, and in a number of other areas. He is now becoming scarce and is not easy to find anywhere.

He prefers rocky, forested hills with open, grassy areas at the top. He wanders about in a herd of as many as twenty animals and can be dangerous if wounded or pursued too closely. He likes to be left strictly alone.

Gaurs are very dark brown in color, sometimes almost black, sometimes with red tones. They almost always have white stockings on all four feet.

The herds graze in the early morning and in the evening, but they prefer to retreat to the thicker parts of the forest during the heat of the day. They can stand quietly for hours and chew their cud and let other, more foolish creatures exert themselves in the sun.

Gaurs like their comfort, their peace, and their quiet. Left alone, they mind their own business and bother no one. Tigers are very fond of their flesh, and the leopard is willing to have a go at a gaur given half a chance. Gaur calves, particularly, are in danger from the great hunting cats. Man has found it great fun to shoot gaurs, and they are listed among the big game of the world. Unfortunately, there has been too much shooting now, and the species may disappear in the wild. They do quite well in zoos, however, so we will probably always have some gaurs around.

It is doubtful that the gaur figured very importantly in the history of our present-day domesticated cattle, if at all, but he is one of the truly great hoofed animals of the world. He is thrilling to behold and gives a private view into what the world must have been like when the gaur's ancestors weren't large animals compared to the rest, but small ones.

The Beaver (*Castor canadensis*)

A Very Important Mammal

A fine study of the European beaver appears on this 1954 Polish stamp. The animal appears to be very life-like, and his setting is clearly displayed.

In 1954 Canada issued a pair of stamps to publicize National Wildlife Week. The walrus appeared on a 4¢ gray stamp and the beaver on this 5¢ ultramarine issue. If you look at this stamp quite closely, you will see that it is really an excellent study of this most interesting animal.

The beaver was once a very important element in the huge Russian fur industry. He is pictured on these two Russian stamps—one from 1961 and the other 1967. I like the style used in the earlier stamp best. You notice the different perspectives or points of view used; in the earlier stamp you are looking down on the beaver, and in the later one you are looking directly at him. It makes a difference.

There is disagreement among scientists as to whether there is one species of beaver or two. Most, though, seem to feel there are two, one in the New World and one in the Old. The beavers are among the largest of the rodents. A big male can weigh a very impressive seventy pounds and be close to five feet long, including over a foot of tail. They are still found in many parts of the United States and Canada, although in nowhere near the numbers there once were. In Europe they still survive in the Elbe River in Germany, the Rhone Valley in France, and in parts of Poland, Sweden, Norway, Finland, and Russia. That they have survived anywhere at all is a near miracle.

The beaver was important to the history of the United States and Canada. In Europe his pelt was considered valuable, particularly for making felt hats. French fur trappers followed the stories of great beaver populations westward and opened up new territory in the search. Rivers were charted, colonies founded, and regions explored because of the lure of the beaver. Empires were built on the fortunes earned from the sale of beaver pelts. Beavers were hunted and hunted and hunted until it suddenly seemed as if none would be left in a matter of years, if not months. Then, just as suddenly as it had started, the assault stopped. The value of the pelt dropped on the European market, wildlife protection came into force, and the beaver has bounced right back just as if he were made of rubber.

Everyone knows that the beavers are the great builders of the animal kingdom. They build dams that can block rivers—sometimes a dam will be nearly half a mile long—and they create their own lakes and ponds. In the middle of these artificial bodies of water, they build their homes with the entrance and exit underwater. Inside these fine homes of sticks and mud, there is a dry shelf well above the waterline. Amazingly, no matter what the temperature outside, the temperature inside is constant and beaver-comfortable. These industrious little animals then cut a supply of their favorite food and store it underwater where they can get at it even if the pond freezes over. With their world all neatly arranged, the beavers are ready to relax for the winter and take care of their needs far from prying eyes or biting winter winds.

If a beaver cuts down a tree too far from the edge of his private lake, he will build a small dam, create a private canal, and float the log to where he needs it. And he does all of these thing without a college degree in engineering!

When we say that the beaver is an important animal, we don't mean just because of his fur. The beaver changes the world around him, and many other animals benefit from his labor. The moose likes to browse at the edge of the beaver pond, and many ducks find breeding places there as well. The ponds the beaver makes and the trees he cuts create forest clearings. When the dams finally collapse, sometimes years after they are built, a clearing results that is a delight to the white tail and mule deer. Many other animals benefit as well from the skill and energy of the beaver, the cleverest of the rodents, master builder of the animal kingdom.

The Lynx (*Lynx* sp.)

Cat of the Northlands

This 1954 stamp from Yugoslavia carries a dramatic portrait of a lynx. It is part of a set, which also featured the red deer, bear, chamois, pelican, black beetle, bush cricket, black lizard, salamander, and trout. In 1956 the sea horse, paper nautilus, rock lobster, sea perch, red mullet, scorpion fish, and wrasse were added. In 1960, the hedgehog, squirrel, marten, hare, fox, badger, wolf, roe deer, and wild boar joined this interesting parade.

A very disagreeable-looking lynx glowers at us from this 1965 Polish stamp. It may not be the best painting of a lynx that was ever done, but it is characteristic in its pose, and the background is suitable. It is a big, good-looking stamp.

The Spanish lynx is a very seriously endangered animal and may be facing extinction in our time. This 1972 Spanish stamp pictures its rare cat. It is a very pleasing stamp, and it is important that stamps call our attention to those animals most in need of our help.

This 1967 stamp from Israel features the caracal, a form of lynx. This stamp reflects Israel's determination to restore the wildlife of Biblical times.

(for the Spanish lynx only) VANISHING ANIMAL

In the rather large and varied cat family, there is a small group of cats known as the lynx. There are four species in this group: the Canadian lynx of Canada and the United States; the European lynx, once found over most of northern Europe but now much restricted in range; the bobcat of the United States, southern Canada, and parts of Mexico; and the caracal of Africa and southern Asia.

Altogether, these cats are among the fiercest on earth. They are matched by a few others like the European wildcat (sometimes confused in people's minds with the lynx) but surpassed by none. Although a somewhat small cat, seldom reaching two feet at the shoulder and not often weighing more than thirty pounds, the lynx is as tough as they come. You have perhaps heard the expression, "He can lick his weight in bobcats!" Well, such a man never existed, for a hundred and fifty pounds of bobcat or lynx would be much more than any man could take on!

The lynx is sometimes confused with the bobcat, but the two animals are really quite easy to tell apart. The lynx is larger and has very prominent ear tufts and a black-tipped tail. The bobcat doesn't have ear tufts that he can boast about, and his tail has black bars but no black tip. Both animals have soft, thick fur that varies quite a bit in tone. There are buffs, grays, reds, and tans all mixed in with sometimes a real salt-and-pepper look. There are spots and bars of darker tones on a very much lighter belly. The lynx has feet that you would think would do for a cat three times his size. He needs them for walking on snow.

Both bobcat and lynx will eat any mammal or bird they can kill. The lynx depends on the snowshoe hare for most of his food, while the bobcat tends to have more variety in his diet.

It takes sixty days for the mother lynx to produce her young, who generally appear in the very early spring. Anywhere from one to four young will be found in a litter. They live on their mother's milk for about two months but stay with her to benefit from her skill for six to nine months altogether. The mother lynx makes a good teacher-protector. When she has young with her, she can be even shorter-tempered than usual and will attack a man if necessary to protect her treasured cubs.

Bobcats seem to be more adaptable than the Canadian lynx and have been doing quite well for themselves despite the traps, guns, and poisons that have been mustered against them. They like rocky hillsides, deep semitropical swamps, and do just fine in deserts, too. It is hard to find an area where bobcats can't make their way through life. Unless killed by a bullet or a trap, they can live for ten to twenty years. There will be bobcats about for a long time yet, and that is quite an exciting thought.

The Cheetah (*Acinonyx jubatus*)

Fastest Cat of All

The well-known naturalist and author Gerald Durrell has a nature preserve on the Island of Jersey, in the English Channel. (That is where Jersey cows come from.) Consequently, this Jersey stamp features the cheetah, an endangered species. The year of issue was 1972.

A handsome wildlife set from Poland in 1972 featured this lanky cheetah looking just as he would while walking through the yellow African grass. The Polish name for the cheetah is *gepard*.

Kenya is the home of the cheetah—one of a number of African countries where some of these cats can still be found. This 1966 stamp from that East African country shows the cheetah moving at what is probably top speed through the grass.

This 1972 stamp shows the cheetah in dry country. The set of which this stamp is a part honors the Nature Reserve Authority of Israel.

VANISHING ANIMAL

The cheetah is the swiftest *four-footed* animal in the world, but not the swiftest animal by any means. A canvasback duck can fly at least as fast; the golden eagle and certain falcons and swifts can fly faster than most cheetahs can ever run. How fast does a cheetah travel? That depends on the individual cheetah you are talking about, but some, at least, can hit nearly seventy miles an hour according to some reports. Others, certainly, can do better than sixty.

A cheetah does not have stamina. Those incredible bursts of speed soon use up his available energy, and the spotted hunting cat lies on his side panting, waiting for his wind to return. That one burst of speed is often enough, though, and a healthy cheetah can usually manage to keep himself fed.

The cheetah or "hunting leopard" (he is definitely *not* a real leopard) was once an open plains cat of India, Egypt, Libya, Morocco, and many parts of Africa south of the Sahara. It is plain to see that nature would never have given such speed to a cat that lived in deep forests or jungles. Doing sixty or more miles an hour among trees would be hazardous indeed. No, the cheetah is a cat made for flat open lands not unlike the prairies of North America.

The spotted, tawny cheetah is very long for his size. Although he will seldom be more than three and a half feet high at the shoulder, he is often over seven feet long, including his lengthy tail. He isn't a heavy cat and will seldom weigh much over 125 pounds. He has very distinctive black lines that run from the corner of his eye to his mouth on each side of his muzzle.

The cheetah differs from all other cats in one very important way. He can't draw his claws back into sheaths as can the other felines. In the words of the scientist, his claws are only *partially retractile.*

The cheetah is a gentle cat in captivity, but he really belongs in his natural habitat where he can hunt his food himself in the manner nature prescribed. That food usually consists of the smaller antelopes, but any small mammal or bird is also likely to be taken. Despite their powerful doglike legs and great speed, cheetahs don't run game down any more than necessary. They prefer to get as close as possible before burning up all that energy.

The female cheetah takes up to 95 days to produce her young, although some cubs appear in ten days less than that. Anywhere from one to four cubs are born, and they are carefully cared for by their mother, who eventually teaches them to hunt by stalking, dashing, and leaping.

Cheetahs rarely bother domestic livestock, and attacks on man by unmolested cheetahs are all but unknown. Despite those very important facts, they are hunted and shot by some men and are now very seriously in danger of extinction. Unless laws are enforced that make it a serious crime to destroy one of these magnificent spotted cats, the only cheetahs left a few decades from now will be found in zoos.

The Hyrax (Procaviidae)

Strange Relative of the Giants

Finding a lion or an elephant on a stamp is one thing, but finding some of the strange little creatures of the world pictured is even more exciting and interesting. This 1962 stamp from French Somaliland (now the French Territory of Afars and Issas) features the attractive little animal known to the Bible as the conie and to modern man most often as the dassie or hyrax.

Just because the comparison is so interesting, here are two stamps featuring the hyrax's closest living relative—the elephant. One is an airmail from Ajman—another one of the United Arab Emirates, with a population of 5,000—and the other is a 1957 stamp from what was formerly called French Equatorial Africa, interesting and quite attractive in its own way. We must not think of the hyrax and the elephants as first cousins; about fourth would be more accurate. It is just that there is nothing at all near the hyrax except the elephant—and nothing at all near the elephant except the hyrax. They are relatives by default.

There are about nine different hyraxes or dassies in the world today, though at one time there were more. Although about the size of a rabbit, they are probably the closest relatives the elephant still has on earth!

All the hyraxes in the world (except those in zoos) are found in Africa, Israel, Syria, and Arabia. They are to be found in mountainous country as high as 15,000 feet above sea level. They are seldom much more than a foot long, and their tail is either very tiny or not to be seen at all. They are chunky little animals and can weigh five pounds or thereabouts.

Although all hyraxes seem to be able to climb well enough, there are three species that are truly arboreal. The tree or bush hyraxes are found in the heavily forested regions of central and southern Africa. These particular animals are nocturnal, shunning daylight unless disturbed. They aren't as socially minded as some of their cousins and spend more time alone or in smaller groups. During the day they sleep in tree hollows or in very dense foliage. When they feed at night, they seek leaves, tender buds, young shoots, and insects, but they are very noisy about the whole affair, croaking, screaming, and making a variety of other sounds that gives their location away. That is rather sad, for they make good eating, and a number of native peoples like to know where the dassies can be found.

There are two groups of rock hyraxes found in parts of Africa and in the Sinai Peninsula, Syria, and Israel. Both kinds are far more gregarious than the tree dassies and love to be around crowds of their own kind.

One group of rock hyraxes, the group found in Africa south of Ethiopia and the Congo, are abroad in the day instead of the night. They love to sun themselves on rocky ledges where, unfortunately, pythons, hungry leopards, and eagles know where to look for them. They live in colonies of hundreds of individuals and have great fun chasing each other about among the rocks. They have keen eyesight, and their hearing is sharp as well. Although generally they are quite peaceful creatures, they do know how to bite and can be very brave in their own defense.

The rock hyraxes from the Israel region live in somewhat smaller colonies of a dozen or more individuals. They, too, like to be about during the daylight hours but will also be found snooping around among the rocks when the moon is full and the weather dry and mild.

The Bighorn Sheep (*Ovis* sp.)

Classic Mountaineer

In 1953, Canada issued a small set of three stamps. The 2¢ featured the polar bear, the 3¢ the moose, and this 4¢ stamp the handsome head of a bighorn sheep.

This 1964 issue from Hungary presents a fine study of a bighorn in a challenging pose. Unfortunately, the rifle on the stamp would seem to suggest that the beautiful creature is for killing. Not everyone agrees with that theory, I'm happy to say.

In 1969, France issued a wildlife stamp showing the Mediterranean mouflon sheep in his natural setting. The tiny panda in the lower left-hand corner represents wildlife conservation—the World Wildlife Fund.

Czechoslovakia also has used the mouflon—*Ovis musimon*—on a stamp, and this country has shown a lot of wildlife over the years. This stamp first went into use in 1963.

More than halfway around the world sweeps a mighty arc representing the range of the great bighorn or wild sheep. The tips of the arc lie along the shores of the Mediterranean on one end and in the Rocky Mountains of North America on the other. From southern Europe across the north of China and north toward the Arctic Ocean it goes, joining the new world in Alaska and sweeping down through western Canada and the United States. Along this great arc the world's hunters march, for the wild sheep are among the most prized big-game trophies. Against them are turned the rifles and scopes of the most skilled killers of all! These great bounding animals are more of a challenge to the hunter than even an elephant or a lion, for just to see a sheep you must travel far and long in the roughest country in the world.

The mountain sheep go where few other animals dare wander. Moving with ease and apparently without any nerves, they bound at high speed from rock to rock on the very edge of the highest cliffs. They are said to jump down as much as fifty feet and to run almost straight up sheer rock faces. Their feet have permanent shock-absorbing pads to help in these high-altitude acrobatics. Like all sheep, these animals are vegetarians and eat a variety of grasses, herbs, buds, and other plant matter.

When breeding time comes, the males challenge each other to duels for claim to the harems. While the females stand off with little interest, the males square off and charge at each other at high speed. They crash their great horns together with a sound that is heard miles away as it echoes off canyon walls below. Sooner or later one or the other of the males gives up and goes his way. Usually both animals survive the combat, but on occasion one may be pushed off a ledge to his death.

One of the handsomest wild sheep of all is the mouflon, which is found only on the islands of Corsica and Sardinia. He has been overhunted and has disappeared from the rest of his much larger original range. The handsome urial with his swept-back horns is still found in small pockets in a number of areas: Cyprus, Turkey, Iran, southern Russia, Afghanistan, India, Pakistan, and Tibet. His range, too, has been carved down by barking rifles aided with telescopic sights. The great argali sheep are spread far across Asia; pockets exist in Siberia, Tibet, India, Russia, and Mongolia, always in remote mountain lands.

North of the Arctic Circle, in Siberia, and in many parts of eastern Asia are to be found the Asiatic bighorns, relatives of the great sheep of North America. In Alaska there are the striking white Dall sheep and the handsome and variable stone sheep. The great bighorns reach down across the western United States all the way to Mexico. In each area, the great sheep reign like mountaintop gods. They are like living monuments that appear to be part of the mountain itself when standing still, but like a bit of the wind as their great bounds carry them out of sight.

The Giant Anteater *(Myrmecophaga tridactyla)*

Strange-looking Beast from South America

Ecuador, in 1960, issued a superb wildlife set that featured a tapir, a spectacled bear, a puma, and this fine portrait of a giant anteater. Note the Latin name present on the stamp: *Myrmecophaga tridactyla.* Nothing could be better for the topical collector!

If only all animal stamps looked like this! This magnificent study of a giant anteater appeared in Venezuela in 1963. The scientific name, as well as the common name, make the stamp of even greater interest and value to the collector. This is truly a fine animal stamp from every point of view.

The anteater has fared rather well—he looks good on stamps. This splendid specimen appears on a stamp from Paraguay of 1969—part of a wildlife or fauna set.

In 1959 Colombia issued a fauna set honoring the great scientific explorer Alexander von Humboldt. This stamp shows the giant anteater—or *hormiguero* as he is known in Spanish—arching his tail over his back. Note that extremely long tongue—it is sticky to trap ants, termites, and beetles.

VANISHING ANIMAL

The word *edentata* means "without teeth" and is also the name of a very interesting order of animals. The order includes the anteaters, the sloths, and the armadillos. All are to be found in South, Central, and North America only. "Without teeth" is somewhat misleading, however, for all of the edentates—except the subject of this chapter, the anteater—have some teeth.

There is only one species of giant anteater, found in the swamps and moist forests of Central and South America. He can be close to seven feet long, including his great bushy tail, and he can weigh fifty pounds or more. He is a slender creature or he would weigh much more to go with that great length.

On each front foot the giant anteater has three large claws and one small one. They are immensely powerful and can rip termite and ant nests apart as if they were paper. The giant's tongue can be as much as two feet long, although it is only about three-quarters of an inch in diameter. When he feeds, his long snake-like tongue is coated with a sticky substance and shoots in and out, in and out, bringing ants, eggs, cocoons, and sometimes beetle larvae to the anteater's tube-like snout. Eventually, he gets enough to keep his large body going.

These giants do not climb trees as do some of the smaller anteaters. They swim well, however, and will cross a wide river. Even though they are very powerful diggers, they do not dig burrows for themselves but curl up for privacy in thick vegetation. They put their snouts between their front paws and cover themselves with their huge, bushy tails, just like a blanket.

When trouble starts, the giant anteater likes to be far away. He has a slow, clumsy gallop and uses it to avoid trouble whenever he can. If forced into a tight situation, however, he knows how to defend himself. Up on his hind legs he goes and takes a stance like a human boxer. He spreads his forelegs wide, and anyone coming close is treated to a lightning-fast slash with those great front claws. An animal adversary can be opened up even easier than an ant nest, it seems, and most animals allow the anteater to have his treasured peace and quiet. Some jaguars and pumas, though, and perhaps some giant snakes, have a go at a giant anteater from time to time, but a battle is bound to follow before a meal is gained.

Only one baby at a time is born to the giant anteater, and it takes the mother 190 days to produce it. The baby rides around on its mother's back until she is expecting another baby, and then it is sent on its way. Some giant anteaters are known to have lived as long as fourteen years.

There are few animals in all this world as strange-looking as this giant among the edentates. The striking color combination of black, white, and gray in bold stripes and designs, the tube-like head, the tiny eyes, the funny shape and great umbrella of a tail make these animals favorite zoo specimens. They do quite well in captivity on a diet of eggs and milk beaten together, with meal worms and ground beef added.

The Tapir (*Tapirus*)

Citizen of South America

The 1960 wildlife set from Ecuador featured this stately tapir against the background of a map. It is a very interesting animal stamp and one the topical collector can treasure.

The magnificent 1963 airmail set from Venezuela included this study of some tapirs; one specimen is seen in the water and another on the riverbank. These handsome stamps were printed for the Venezuelan government in Berlin.

Paraguay issued this fine airmail stamp in 1970 featuring an alert-looking tapir. The painting isn't as good as many others we are seeing in this book, but the overall effect is good—the animal looks "right," and that is what is most important.

The Costa Rican government went as far afield as Tokyo to have this interesting portrait of a tapir printed. The stamp is part of an airmail set of 1963.

The hoofed animals of the world are divided into two great orders, the *perissodactyla* (per-iss-o-dack-tilla), the animals with an odd number of toes, and the *artiodactyla* (art-tee-o-dack-tilla), those with an even number of toes. The perissodactyla is the much smaller group and contains only the horses, tapirs, and rhinoceroses. In all of the Western Hemisphere or New World, only the tapirs represent the order. (We have no true wild native horses in America. The wild mustangs of the West are descendants of domestic horses that ran away or were abandoned.)

There are only four tapirs left: the Brazilian tapir from lowland South America, the woolly tapir from South American mountainous areas, Baird's tapir from Central and South America, and the Asiatic tapir from Burma, Thailand, the Indochinese region, Malaysia, and Sumatra. The Asiatic tapir can be easily distinguished; he is blackish in front and back (including all four legs) but has a white band around his midsection. The South and Central American tapirs are dark pretty much all over, although often a little lighter below.

All tapirs are vegetarians, and they can get along in any wooded or grassy area near water. They are great swimmers, waders, splashers, and wallowers. They spend their days in forests and thickets for safety and comfort and come out to feed in more open areas at night. They generally live alone or in pairs and are good hill-climbers, runners, divers, and sliders.

The snout and upper lip of the tapirs stick out into a short, fleshy trunk, and they rather look like small, chunky elephants that didn't quite make it! The tapirs from South and Central America have longer snouts than the kind from Asia. All tapirs have small eyes and erect, oval ears.

A tapir can be more than eight and a half feet long, can stand three and a half feet at the shoulder, and may weigh 650 pounds. That makes a lot of good eating, and both man and predatory animals seek tapir flesh regularly. The great cats, particularly, are enemies of this peaceful, browsing animal. Man and his agriculture, though, are the biggest enemy with which the tapir has to reckon. They aren't easy to catch, however. They are shy and will usually dash into deep water or crash off into the forest if disturbed. They can bite rather effectively, and until they are tame, that is a good thing to remember about captive specimens. They do very well in captivity and soon settle down to a peaceful life with plenty of food and water. They get along well with their keepers and soon breed—producing striped babies, one at a time usually, but sometimes two. It takes a female nearly 400 days to produce her infant. She is a very good mother and doesn't like anyone to come near her baby until it has started to grow well. A well-cared-for tapir can have thirty years of good life.

The Puma (*Felis concolor*)

Cat of Great Range

A strange-looking puma graces this 1960 stamp from Ecuador. He looks as if he were missing one of his front legs! As a matter of fact, he doesn't look good at all. The other studies in the same set are much better —the tapir and the giant anteater, for example.

Far more appealing is the puma on this 1963 Venezuelan stamp, although here again the others in the set are better. Notice how stamps can reflect the differences of opinion that exist among scientists; this stamp gives *Felis concolor* as the scientific name for the animal, while the stamp from Ecuador gives *Puma concolor.* In this case Venezuela is right and Ecuador wrong.

Paraguay's handsome oversized 1969–70 wildlife set included the puma on a rocky overlook. The face in this rendering isn't quite right, but the body is. With just a little more work the artist could have had a first-class painting of this very splendid animal.

A puma stares down from his perch in a tree on this 1960 Argentine stamp with an *official* overprint. That means that this stamp was issued for use by a government agency rather than the general public. The pale ink used on this stamp gives the puma a ghostlike quality. As a matter of fact, the puma has been called a "ghost" by a great many writers who have known this cat's secret ways.

Mountain lion, puma, cougar, panther, painter, mountain screamer, American lion—he has more names than he knows what to do with—and there has been a great deal of nonsense written about him!

The American mountain lion is nothing more (nor less) than a large, successful, powerful cat. He is related to the big cats of Asia and Africa but not as closely as the jaguar—the only really big cat that shares the Western Hemisphere with the mountain lion. They even overlap ranges in many places south of the border.

The mountain lion probably has a greater north-to-south range than any other species of cat. He is found from well up into Canada all the way down through Central America to very nearly the bottom tip of South America. He can be found in high mountain hideouts, on level plains, in deep and almost impenetrable swamps, and in true jungle. Deserts don't hold him back, and neither do the great grassy highlands of central South America. He is everywhere and he is nowhere, for he is the tawny ghost of the world between the Atlantic and Pacific oceans. Because he is such a ghost, his reputation is very confusing.

No one can tell you for certain where the mountain lion can and cannot be found north of Mexico. He has been so ruthlessly hunted and so badly treated that he has learned how to avoid man with great cunning and skill. He is the original now-you-see-it-now-you-don't cat, and there are endless reports of his having been seen in areas where he is supposed to have been extinct for a hundred years. One recent report comes from the Garden State Parkway in New Jersey!

There are probably very few mountain lions left in the United States east of the Mississippi River. There may be some in New Brunswick in eastern Canada, but nobody knows for certain. The mountain lion may, in fact, be expanding his range again now that the deer herds are back, for he follows the deer, probably his most important single source of food.

The mountain lion, of course, eats only meat and kills what he needs, seldom more. Like most cats he prefers not to waste energy and just can't be bothered with legendary killing sprees. He hunts, kills, eats, rests; then he hunts again. In an area where he is not troubled by men and dogs, he will return again and again to his kill until it is all used up.

He is a solitary kind of cat, this mountain lion of ours, and will often wander far in a single night over what may be a perfectly huge private hunting range. He doesn't like intruders.

The legends that came out of the woods years back that said the mountain lion can scream like a woman are true, although for a while it was thought that these were just nonsense tales like so many others. The mountain lion can make a perfectly terrible noise when he really puts his mind to it. Generally, though, you would never know he was around since he can be extremely quiet as well.

The Musk Ox *(Ovibos moschatus)*

Great One of the Far North

National Wildlife Week in Canada has often called for the appearance of a couple of new wildlife stamps. In 1955 whooping cranes and this head of a musk ox turned up to delight topical collectors.

The musk ox has no really close relatives. About as close as you can get is the takin (whose head is shown on the 1966 stamp from Bhutan), the saiga (on the long, flat 1959 stamp from Mongolia), and the ibex (on the 1970 Jordanian stamp honoring game protection). Other relatives are the chamois, the serow, the mountain goat (see page 78), the goral, the antelopes, and the tahr. None are really very close, but they are as close as you can get. It is possible to construct a family tree of the animal kingdom using stamps for illustrations.

French-speaking Canadians call him *bouefsmusques*, but to most others he is just the good old plain musk ox. Long before man began writing his history down, the musk ox was exterminated in Europe and Siberia, where he once roamed in good numbers. Long before that, animals that were probably identical to present-day musk oxen roamed throughout Germany, France, England, and the United States. Today, this funny, mixed-up creature can be found only in northern Canada and Greenland.

The musk ox is mixed up because he is related to cattle, goats, antelopes, buffaloes, bison, and a host of other animals but isn't very much like any of them. He can be all of eight feet long and can weigh as much as 900 pounds, and he knows how to throw that weight around if his herd is molested.

Musk oxen normally travel in herds of up to a hundred members. When threatened, the herd forms itself into a ring with the young huddled into the center. A wolf or bear finds itself faced with a threatening wall of lowered heads, sharp and ready hoofs, and pointed and waiting horns. Shoulder to shoulder, a herd will stand against all comers, the animals' instincts dictating that the young must be protected at all costs. Sometimes that cost is very high. While wolves find it all but impossible to score against a wall or ring of musk oxen, some so-called sportsmen have found it wonderfully convenient. Since the adults will hold their ground rather than flee and expose the young to danger, these men, who think they are great hunters, find it an easy matter to sit and slaughter as many as they want, so the musk oxen can be easily exterminated in what is left of their range.

Because he has two coats, the musk ox can stand the long, terrible, harsh Arctic winter with its fierce storms. The coarse guard hairs reach nearly to the ground and are great for shedding snow and sleet. Under the guard hairs lies a rich, thick undercoat of light brown hair that is so dense that no cold, no matter how severe, can penetrate.

Mature bulls are very jealous of the females and drive the young bulls away before they can challenge them for leadership. Eventually the young males grow enough to return and take up the battle. Sooner or later the older bulls are driven off their thrones and forced to leave the herd and live out their lives as solitary animals. It is then that they are vulnerable to attack by wolves. It is then that they fall, but not without a roaring good fight. More than one wolf has paid with his life for attempting to gain a musk ox steak.

The musk ox eats only vegetable matter. When the snow is thick on the ground, he seeks out areas where the wind has blown with particular fury. In these areas, where the snow lies most shallow, he digs down with his front hoofs for grass, moss, and lichens. Harsh as it is, the Arctic suits the musk ox just fine.

The Mountain Goat (*Oreamnos americanus*)

Daredevil of the High Places

The North American mountain goat is a rare animal on stamps, but in 1956 Canada issued two stamps for National Wildlife Week, one picturing a mountain goat and one a caribou. This appears to be a wise old billy who is staring right back at us from the stamp. It seems as if he knows something we don't know!

Here are two studies of his European counterpart—the chamois. One is from Spain in 1972, where the chamois is known as *rebeco,* and the other from Czechoslovakia in 1963, where they call him *kamzik.* The North American mountain goat and the chamois are related and have something in common—each is the only species within its genus. A genus is the next scientific grouping up from species. Some genera (that is plural for genus) have dozens of species—but these two (*Oreamnos* for the mountain goat and *Repicapra* for the chamois) have just one each. The animals have similar habits and habitats.

The great North American mountain goat is not a true goat at all. He is what is best described as a goat-antelope. He is the acrobat of the high places and at times is even more of a daredevil than the bighorn sheep. He is seldom seen in anything but rocky mountaintops and rarely below the timberline. He can go where no other large animal can, and he can go there with apparent grace and ease.

There is only one species of mountain goat, and in the United States he is found in the Rocky Mountains, in Montana, Idaho, and in parts of Oregon. He is found as well up through parts of western Canada into Alaska.

A mountain goat can be five to six feet long and can weigh as much as 250 pounds, sometimes even more. He is white or yellowish white and has very, very thick, woolly fur. His horns are often shiny black.

Despite their weight, the goats can pick their way along ledges only a couple of inches wide. Many animals would like to get at them for their ample flesh, but few ever have a chance. Some kids may be killed by wolves, bears, mountain lions, and even eagles, but adults are seldom molested.

There is one great danger in the high places where the mountain goat wanders, and he can do little to protect himself against it. An exceptional heavy snowfall or the onset of the spring thaw can cause a snow slide. It is believed that more mountain goats are thrown to their death in avalanches than are killed by any other means. Since they generally travel in small bands or family units, more than one goat may be swept away over a cliff to his death when a wall of snow suddenly gives way.

One or two kids are born between April and June and can stand within ten minutes of their birth. Within twenty minutes they are happily nursing, and from that moment on they stay very close to their mothers. In less than an hour after being born a mountain goat kid can actually jump.

As might be expected, mountain goats are considered game by the "sportsmen" of the world. Armed with extremely high-powered rifles and telescopic scopes, these determined hunters mount the canyon walls and scramble up long and wearying slopes. To their credit, it must be said that they at least are willing to go far, work hard, and risk dangers as well as discomfort in order to take their prey. Still, it is unfortunate that so many mountain goats must die for no good reason at all.

No one knows for sure how many of these great mountaineers there are left in the world, but there are certainly fewer than there were just a few years ago. Since they live in such remote places, they will probably continue to survive. It is nice to know that they are there, adorning the mountain with a patch of living white against the dead gray of the frozen rocks.

The Sloth (*Bradypus* and *Choloepus*)

No Great Need for Speed

The interesting wildlife set that appeared in Venezuela in 1963 included this family group of sloths. Notice that the animal on the right is a female and that she is clutching her baby in her arms. It helps to have a powerful magnifying glass handy when you look at stamps since there can be a great deal of detail crammed into a small space.

The three-toed sloth appears on this 1959 Colombian stamp—part of a set honoring the German explorer of South America, Alexander von Humboldt. (They named the Humboldt Current and the Humboldt penguin after him, among other things.) On this stamp a sloth or *unau* honors his memory. This is the position in which a sloth is happiest.

The old three-toed—upside down as usual—appears on this nice fauna stamp from Paraguay in 1969–1970. Paraguay isn't a very big or a very rich country—the population is only about 12,600,000—and these handsome stamps (for collectors more than letter-writers) are an important source of income.

(for the three-toed sloth only)

VANISHING ANIMAL

There are two different kinds of sloths in this world, and both come from the same general area. The smaller three-toed sloth is found in the forests of Honduras all the way south through Argentina, Paraguay, and Brazil. He is usually about two and half feet long and weighs up to ten pounds. The somewhat larger two-toed sloth can be a few inches longer but can weigh twice as much. He is found in the forests of Venezuela, Guyana, Surinam, French Guiana, and northern Brazil; another species is found in adjacent areas from Nicaragua down into Brazil and even Peru.

When you stop to think about it, it is a miracle that the sloth survives in this world at all since he lives in a jungle where many enemies roam. The sloth's hearing and eyesight are quite poor, and only by smell and touch can he find his way around and get food to keep going. On top of that, he can't walk! A sloth on level ground can get around only by hooking his great, long claws into something and pulling himself along. He spends his life hanging upside down in the trees, and only then is he happy. Some sloths, it is believed, spend their entire lives in a single tree.

Everything a sloth does is slow. It is almost like watching a slow-motion movie. Shoot off a gun nearby, and a sloth takes what seems to be hours just to turn his head and look in the direction of the disturbance. As he progresses along a branch in search of food, a sloth slowly moves one great hooked paw out in front of another and swings his body forward only when a safe purchase on the branch has been made. The whole process, like everything else he does, is painfully slow.

Surprisingly, a sloth swims well and does not hesitate to take to water if pressed. He can fight, amazingly enough, and although not exactly a whirling dervish, he can cause wicked injuries if he catches someone with his hooked claws. Generally, though, a sloth is happy only when being left strictly alone. You can hardly accuse a sloth of going around looking for trouble.

Both kinds of sloths are leaf-eaters in the natural state. They pull bunches of leaves toward their mouths in slow motion and quietly, slowly munch away.

The three-toed sloth can produce young in as few as 120 days, although 150 or so is probably nearer to average. It takes the two-toed version more than 250 days. In both cases twins are rare, one being the usual number of young. They probably live upward of fifteen years if left unmolested.

A certain number of sloths must fall prey to jaguars and pumas. There are also giant snakes in their natural haunts, and it would seem that some boa constrictors and anacondas must enrich their diets on sloths. It is difficult to see how a sloth could outwit a big cat or outbattle a twenty-foot constrictor.

The sloths are truly among the oddest mammals in the world. They don't bother anybody, and if you were to look carefully at the expression on the average sloth's face, you would be convinced that practically nothing bothers him.

The Tarsier (*Tarsius* sp.)

Strange Little Tree-Dweller

Sarawak, a state of Malaysia, located in the northwestern part of the island of Borneo bordering on the South China Sea, embraces an area of 50,000 square miles. In this portrait of a tarsius—which appeared in 1950—somehow the ghostlike quality of this night animal comes through to us.

In 1969 the Republic of the Philippines showed the tarsier on this rather handsome stamp. It stands very alert on a thick stalk of bamboo as though it has seen an arboreal snake or heard an owl call. Note the broad finger pads so useful for gripping a tree—like suction cups.

Confusion is always possible in classifying animal stamps. These two stamps feature the potto, which is related to the tarsier but quite different. Note how much smaller the ears are! Both stamps are from Africa—one from the Congo (1971) and the other from Rio Muni, a province of Equatorial Guinea (1967).

The primates, the highest order of animals on our planet, are made up of a variety of animals ranging from extremely primitive forms like the tree shrew all the way up to man. Part way up the ladder, but nowhere near the top, is a family known as the *Tarsiidae*. They are strange little creatures, and in all the world there are only three species. Tarsiers have been around for a very, very long time. They are an extemely ancient group of primates, perhaps the most ancient of all.

All of our planet's tarsiers live on southwest Pacific islands, on Sumatra, Borneo, the Philippines, and others we seldom hear of. It is in places like Banka, Billiton, Karimata, Natuna, Savu, Pulo Peleng, and Bohol that the tarsiers are found. They themselves are as enchanting as the names of their island homes.

A tarsier may be as much as seventeen inches long, but only a third of that will be head and body; the rest is very skinny tail. A really fat tarsier will weigh a crushing total of five ounces. As you might guess, tarsiers aren't very dangerous animals! When you look at a tarsier, the things you see first, and generally look at longest, are the eyes. They are truly immense, for the tarsier is a creature of the night and needs to gather as much light as possible.

How do some of these strange animals get their names? Why call anything a *tarsier*? There is more sense to these names than many people realize. The tarsier has very long or *elongated* hind legs. The very much elongated section is known in anatomy as the ankle or *tarsal region*, hence tarsier.

The tarsier not only prefers night to day; he also prefers the trees and bushes to the ground. He can get around on the ground quite well and can jump as far as five feet or more and as high as two feet, but he feels safer on branches and among leaves. He can really jump when he is branch-hopping and loves to exercise his wonderful ability as an acrobat.

Not only does this little primate have good eyesight, he has sharp hearing as well. His paper-thin ears are seldom still but are constantly adjusting to the sounds of the world around. He can turn his head nearly all the way around without moving his body, so he has a wonderful field of vision. He is very alert to danger, and when not well hidden in a hollow tree or in a thick clump of vegetation, he is constantly checking things out to make certain that no enemies are around.

Insects make up the bulk of the tarsier's diet, although he will not turn up his nose at a tasty lizard now and then. When he spots his prey, he leaps, quickly catching his dinner in both his front paws. They are amazingly like human hands and can grasp things very firmly.

A newborn tarsier may weigh as little as half an ounce but is quite well developed. He is born with his eyes open and is capable almost immediately of making short leaps and of traveling with his mother by clinging to her fur.

The Orangutan *(Pongo pygmaeus)*

Old Man of the Forest

This baby orangutan first appeared in 1955, sharing this issue from Sarawak with Queen Elizabeth II. He appears to be very intent on going about his business, whatever it might be.

The orangutan hasn't appeared on very many postage stamps, which is strange. Although his range is small on this planet, the orang has been popular in zoos and is now a seriously endangered species. At any rate, here is another—this one from the Republic of Indonesia. The portrait looks better when you use a magnifying glass. The year of issue was 1959.

This old stamp—it appeared first in 1899—from North Borneo (now Sabah) has a rather silly portrait of an orangutan. He looks more like a hairy man than a great ape. Animal art wasn't at its best in 1899—and neither was stamp design. If you look very closely, you will see that there are three other orangs in this picture.

At the very top of the primate order is man, and just below that strange mammal come the great apes, which are few in number—half a dozen species of gibbons, one species of chimpanzee, one of gorilla, and one of orangutan. These few apes are the world's full and final allotment, and there will never be any more.

The orangutan is one of the world's seriously endangered species. He doesn't do well when his environment is altered, and he has no defense against guns, bows, and spears. Unless he is given some quick and important consideration, one of the world's most exciting big animals will suddenly be no more.

All of the wild orangutans in the world now live on two islands, Sumatra and Borneo. They grow to be quite large creatures, and a big male can measure between five and six feet, head and body included. His arms reach down to his ankles, and when he extends them to the sides, his total spread may be close to eight feet. Orangutans get very, very fat in their old age, and an old male can weigh nearly 300 pounds. They are the second largest ape. The gorilla is first with no dispute.

It takes an orangutan mother about as long to produce her baby as it does a human mother, nine months. A newborn baby will weigh about four pounds and be completely helpless. The mother may keep her baby on milk for as long as *six years*. The offspring are fully grown in about a dozen years and may live to be as much as forty.

Orangutans eat mostly fruit, although leaves, seeds, bark, eggs, and even young birds are sometimes included on the jungle menu. At night, the great apes build themselves vine and stick nests high in the trees, where they sleep in comfort and safety. The higher they can go, the happier they are. If the rain starts to fall in the middle of the night, the orang will reach out and pull in some leaves to use as blankets. He doesn't particularly enjoy being wet.

An orangutan likes nothing so much as his peace. If left alone, he bothers nobody. He has a mild curiosity and will come close to look things over, but that is the limit of his natural aggression. In the trees he moves along easily by hanging from his arms or by walking along branches and grasping with his powerful feet. When an animal moves along under a branch by reaching hand over hand, we call that *brachiating*. On the ground an orangutan walks on all fours, resting on the knuckles of his hands. He is seldom in much of a hurry unless his small family group is threatened.

Just how smart is an orangutan? Most people have been led to believe that chimpanzees are the geniuses of the ape world. That would appear to be so because they are natural clowns and show-offs and will do anything to attract and hold attention. The gorillas and the orangutans are not so inclined. They don't care whether everyone thinks that they are great or not. They don't respond to tests and tricks and regard the whole business as a big bore. Therefore, they just don't appear to be bright. That is misleading, however, for every indication is that the gorilla and the orangutan are just as smart as any chimpanzee.

The Gerenuk (*Litocranius walleri*)

An Unlikely-looking Animal

The French Somaliland (now the French Territory of the Afars and the Issas) wildlife set of 1958 included these gerenuks as well as a wart hog and a cheetah. This is a particularly clean and graceful stamp.

Ethiopia featured the head of a gerenuk in 1919. Animal stamps go far back in the history of postage, and it is still fairly easy to get even some of the earlier examples. This portrait isn't the best one in the world, but it is nice to find our long-necked friend on such an old stamp.

In 1967, using a modern treatment (compare it to the Ethiopian stamp), Somalia gave us a lightly tripping gerenuk. It is more of a cartoon character that we see here than a flesh-and-blood animal, but it is a happy stamp—at least the animal looks happy.

It is easy to make a mistake when the scientific names aren't present. On this stamp from the Republic of Togo in 1957 the animal is the kob—French name, *cobe de buffon*. There is a similarity in the horns, and these stamps make the kob look lighter in body than he actually is. But confusion is easy, and some collectors have thought this was a gerenuk.

The family Bovidae (*bo-videe*) contains some enchanting-looking animals. All of the cattle, buffaloes, and antelope come together under this heading, and the variety appears to be almost endless. Buried in the middle of this vast array of wildlife is a single species of a particularly strange-looking animal known to science as *Litocranius walleri*, to Africans as gugufto or nanjaat, and to English-speaking peoples as the gerenuk.

The gerenuk or giraffe-gazelle is found in eastern Africa, particularly in dry scrub areas. From the French Territory of the Afars and the Issas to Kenya, in country most like desert, this strange creature will be found living his quiet, inoffensive life.

The gerenuk is between five and six feet long, including his nine- to ten-inch tail. He can stand a little over three feet at the shoulder but will seldom weigh more than a hundred pounds. He is quite slender and easily distinguished by his very long, giraffe-like neck. It is not only a long neck but also a skinny one. It is usually no more than ten inches around. The male gerenuk, and the male only, has rather impressive horns. They can be more than a foot in length.

Gerenuks live on vegetable matter, with acacia leaves being of foremost importance. They stand upright on their hind legs to reach the top branches where the tender, young leaves grow. Often, however, particularly in arid regions, dried or wilted leaves and twigs have to do. The gerenuk doesn't seem to mind. Where water is available, the gerenuk may drink. In some areas, though, he may never drink at all but rather get his moisture from his food. In effect, the tree drinks for him.

If we are to be perfectly honest, it cannot be said for certain that the gerenuk adorns the stamps illustrating this chapter. The animal pictured may be the dibatag or Clarke's gazelle. It is not always possible to tell by looking at a stamp!

The dibatag, like the gerenuk, lives in eastern Africa and seems to prefer the same kind of dry country. He is about five feet long, about three feet at the shoulder, and weighs about 75 pounds. He is not too different in appearance, although perhaps a little lighter than his cousin the gerenuk. His horns are a chief distinguishing characteristic, and on the stamp from what was formerly French Somaliland, there is a touch of the dibatag about the buck feeding on the acacia tree.

One way of telling the dibatag from the gerenuk in the field is by the way they run. The dibatag runs with his head arched back and his tail thrown forward. The gerenuk runs with his head and tail stretched out flat.

It is a little surprising that nature made two such similar animals to live in the same general area and perform the same general function. However, although they are similar, it must be remembered that they are two quite separate and distinct animals. Both, apparently, are preyed upon by the leopard, although their fast, graceful paces must make them tough prey to capture unless ambushed.

The Paca *(Cuniculus paca)*

Giant Rodent of South America

One of the most handsome and successful of the stamps in the 1963 Venezuelan wildlife set is this study of the paca at the foot of a giant tree.

The Costa Rican triangular airmail set of 1963 that was printed in Tokyo included this study of the paca. Notice that in Costa Rica the paca is known as *tepescuintle,* while in Venezuela he is *la lapa.*

Guyana featured the paca on this high-denomination stamp in 1968. In this South American country the animal is known as *labba.* You can learn something about language by studying postage stamps!

This 1971 large and splendid stamp from Trinidad and Tobago has a very handsome painting of the *lappe* or the paca. It is a finely done rendering, and the animal looks very natural, very alert. These animals are either alert or dead.

When someone says "rodent," most people immediately think of rats and mice. If they think a little deeper and a little longer, they come up with squirrels, groundhogs, beavers, prairie dogs, and several other animals. Few people, however, seem to realize that there are some very large rodents in this world and that some of them really don't look like rats and mice at all.

Such a group of "giants" is the family *Dasyproctidae* (*Dass-ee-prock-ti-dee*), animals from Central and South America. Included in the family are agoutis, acushis, and pacas. The pacas are the largest of all, and an adult male may be over thirty-two inches long and can weigh between twenty and twenty-five pounds. That is a big mouse!

The paca has a very, very short tail, and it will not be noticed at all unless you look for it. The body is brownish or blackish, and there are usually four rows of white dots or spots along each side. All the pacas of the world live somewhere between Mexico and southern Brazil and prefer forested areas, particularly when water is at hand.

Pacas swim very well and take to water when danger threatens. It is a favorite escape route. They generally live alone and spend their days underground in burrows, which they dig for themselves in riverbanks, along slopes, in a rock jumble, or among a mass of roots. They make several escape hatches for themselves and usually keep their busy, twitching noses below ground and out of sight during the day since they are strictly nocturnal.

When dusk settles over the pacas' forest or jungle homes, they emerge into the moist, clinging air and travel along favorite and well-worn paths to customary watering and feeding places. A great variety of stems, leaves, roots, and fruit is eaten. Mangoes and avocados are favorites, and when they fall to the ground, that is where the pacas will be found.

The paca has a funny chamber built into his skull unlike anything found in other mammals. It is a kind of sound box or *resonating chamber* and makes his voice sound very much stronger than it really is. When angry, the paca growls quite convincingly.

Where the paca lives, there are big cats, the jaguar and the mountain lion; some small cats, the ocelot and the margay; and a variety of very large snakes, perhaps the largest snakes in the world. In the rivers and streams there are members of the crocodile family, the cayman. All of these predators are enemies of the paca, and this little vegetarian must be constantly alert. It is believed that a paca can live close to twenty years. It is an alert animal that makes it all the way!

As if he didn't have enough to worry about, the paca has been blessed (or cursed!) with very tasty flesh. Natives of the countries where he is found pay high prices for him in the butcher shops, and paca meat is considered a favored delicacy. Thus, the paca has more than his fair share of problems. Somehow, though, nature seems to have provided enough pacas to go around, and they are doing very well in their tropical homes.

The Fennec (*Fennecus zerda*)

A Fox with Big Ears

In 1962 the country then called French Somaliland issued this engaging double portrait of two dainty fennecs. It is one of my favorite wildlife stamps.

The fennec's almost unbelievable ears are very apparent in this 1951 semipostal from Ifni (now part of Morocco). The animal itself, however, is nowhere near so pleasing as on the French Somaliland issue.

Sometimes a country will honor an animal on a whole set. A four-stamp set from Spanish Sahara (1970) shows the fennec in a number of different poses, two of which are shown here. If Spanish Sahara actually used all the stamps they issued for outgoing mail, the whole country would do nothing but sit around and write all day. These stamps were not actually intended to adorn envelopes; they were issued for sale to collectors.

The *canines* or dog family consists of a number of particularly interesting animals often very different in appearance from their near cousins. Included in the group are the domestic dogs, wolves, coyotes, jackals, foxes, fennecs, so-called raccoon-dogs, small-eared dogs, bush dogs, dholes, hunting dogs, and several other forms as well. One of the most intriguing of all, and certainly one of the most enchanting to look at, is the fennec or fennec fox.

The fennecs are found in the desert regions of northern Africa and on the Sinai and Arabian peninsulas. In the United States the fennec has relatives or *counterparts* known as the swift or kit fox.

These little creatures from the dry world around the southern and eastern shores of the Mediterranean Sea are the smallest foxes in the world, and the palest colored as well. A big fennec can be two and a half feet long, almost half of that being a reasonably bushy tail. He will weigh about four pounds, or about as much as a small toy poodle to which he is very distantly related—both are canines.

The fennec's most outstanding characteristic, literally, is the size of his ears. They are huge! They can be as much as six and half or seven inches long. The animal itself is a pale reddish cream to almost a white in color, with a distinct black tip to his tail.

Fennecs are usually active only at night. One good reason for this is the extreme heat of the desert day. They dig burrows into the sand with astounding speed and there hide until the sun is down. Their food preferences vary, but eggs, lizards, and insects are probably favored. When fennec tracks are found near water, they are seen to lead back and forth, so it can be assumed that fennecs drink. However, their tracks are often found so far from the nearest oasis that it can also be assumed that they don't have to. Like a great many animals that live in desert regions, they apparently drink when and if water is available. At other times they get enough moisture from their food.

Fennecs probably live about as long as most dogs do, from ten to fifteen years. They produce their young in about fifty days, and anywhere from one to five kits will be born at a time. The mothers take very good care of their babies and can be quite courageous in their defense.

Shy and alert, quick and ghostly, these little big-eared foxes of the North African desert country are a delight to behold. It is fun to think of them living out their lives even if we don't get to see them very often. Somehow, in some mysterious way, nature decided that she needed another little mammal, another little wild member of the dog family to fill a task in the desert lands north of rich central Africa. She molded the fennec out of the special clay of evolution and taught it how to survive where others could not. Truly, it is a wonderful world we live in, particularly the world of mammals.

Index of Countries Represented